SIGIL CRAFT

SIGIL CRAFT

YOUR GUIDE TO USING, CREATING & RECOGNIZING MAGICKAL SYMBOLS

By Lia Taylor

STERLING ETHOS
New York

STERLING ETHOS
New York

An Imprint of Sterling Publishing Co., Inc.
122 Fifth Avenue
New York, NY 10011

ISBN 978-1-4549-4693-9 (hardcover)
ISBN 978-1-4549-4694-6 (e-book)

Library of Congress Control Number: 2023932086

For information about custom editions, special sales, and premium purchases,
please contact specialsales@unionsquareandco.com.

Printed in the U.S.A.

2 4 6 8 10 9 7 5 3 1

unionsquareandco.com

Cover design by Melissa Farris

Interior design by Gavin Motnyk

Cover and interior illustrations by Lia Taylor

To my dad

Robert Edward Taylor (1952–2021)

CONTENTS

PREFACE

Before we begin, I wish to touch base on a couple of matters regarding magic. While the focus of this book is sigils, the language is inevitably twisted and woven into the language of magic and witchcraft on a whole. The views in this book are my own, based on months (and sometimes years) of research and study, or based on personal experience and my own point of view. Take what you need from this book, and leave the rest.

ON MAGIC(K)

The spelling *magick* with a *k* was popularized by Aleister Crowley, to distinguish the arcane arts from the art of illusion performed by stage magicians. Day-to-day, I use various spellings interchangeably. I think that any and all spellings have merit, and sometimes one spelling feels more in line with the topic at hand.

Magick, *magic*, *magike*, and *magix* are all sides of the same metaphysical die. For simplicity's sake, I use the words magick and magic in this book.

ON GENDER IN MAGIC

Hi, it's me, your friendly neighborhood nonbinary witch. I'm not interested in practicing magic in binary ways, or gendering everything. However, I am interested in historical accuracy, and gender has a place within that framework. In some historical contexts, it is relevant to discuss how gender plays a part in the history of the occult and witchcraft. As a nonbinary person, I'm interested in gender studies, the history of gender equality, and where I would have (and do) fit as neither/both masculine and feminine.

Magic is queer, and we should explore it as such. It's important to acknowledge that the history of magic and the history of our planet have a lot of queerness, in spite of centuries and millennia of attempted erasure.

My opinion and view of gender (including the gender binary) are constantly evolving and shifting. I don't think that there should be any shame in admitting that we as individuals and a society are in a constant state of flux, shifting and forming ideas, experimenting and unlearning. We're generally pretty quick to react when someone doesn't share the same opinion or doesn't have the same information. We're open and willing to have discussions with others—until the other doesn't share our views or understanding. In a hundred years (heck, even ten years), the way I discuss gender in this book may be obsolete and embarrassing. That doesn't mean that there's anything inherently wrong with my views at the time I'm writing this. It's how I currently see the world and my understanding of the world, and that perception is constantly shifting. Even my understanding of magic and witchcraft will change drastically in the near future. Part of being a curious magic maker is holding the willingness to experiment and grow, and acknowledging that we don't always have the answers.

Some of my complicated views around gender exist because of the dialogues created in most magic books. Magicians and witches, like most humans, are not always the most flexible when it comes to shifting beliefs or looking at their beliefs in objective ways. It's really hard to find a comfortable space to explore your gender and your identity when every book you read is seemingly very rigid in how things are "supposed to be." Western magic and occult systems are largely built on binaries, including definitions that involve the masculine and feminine, and how those concepts exist in relation to each other. In alchemy, there are some ideas around the androgynous and hermaphroditic, but even then, it is still born out of the goal of marrying two opposing and complementary ideas. There's not a lot of room for exploring the "other." If you're not introduced to other ideas, how are you supposed to ever explore or expand your individual identity or magic systems as a whole?

In a lot of magical texts (even books being written now), a lot of ideas distill gender down to female = vulva/womb, and male = penis, which isn't true. It's easy to see why people become dismissive of these books. It's a slippery slope toward trans-exclusionary radical feminist (TERF) ideals, which can be incredibly harmful. The intention may never be intended to harm (sometimes the defenses for these ideals border on saviorism), but there is a very famous phrase about the road to hell and what it is paved with.

When I started writing this book, I was adamant that I wouldn't discuss gender outside of historical contexts, because I personally don't see the value of using the traditional gendering of things and concepts, like planets, plants, crystals, and anything else that may be a correspondence. As I was working on the correspondence section, however, I was reminded that my experience in this realm is not the same as others'. For some people, the dualities of masculine and feminine can be helpful. It's really not up to me to decide, and it's a little unreasonable of me to discuss themes of openness and curiosity and working outside of dichotomies, but then be really adamant that *this one thing* isn't okay.

I encourage everyone to see how they can work outside of the gender binary and remove gendering from places that don't call for it. I encourage exploration, intuition, and curiosity when it comes to magic. But this doesn't mean you're forbidden from using these traditional associations and correspondences that are based on masculine and feminine concepts. I had the realization that maybe I was being dismissive of nonbinary ideas around the "both" (embodying masculine and feminine aspects) and maybe being more dismissive around ideas of using magic to find comfort and clarity for trans individuals. Not every trans person is nonbinary, just as not all nonbinary people are trans. I suspect that using the idea of masculine and feminine within magic could be extremely beneficial in combating body or gender dysmorphia. There are reasonable and valid ways of working with the gender binary through magic and the metaphysical to help ourselves.

ON DEMONS AND OTHER ENTITIES

Throughout this book I'll use words like *demons*, but whenever possible, I will choose to use the word *spirits*. In certain contexts, the word *demon* makes sense, given the context in which we're discussing it, but I don't like implying that demons are inherently bad. Back in Greece, the word *daimon* was ambiguous, referring to spirits and lesser gods. Even the Latin word *daemon* means spirit. It wasn't until the Christianization of Europe that the word *demon* started to take on negative connotations.

Did you know that the definition of the word *hex* only means "to cast spells," and that the word *god* is not gendered? Language is a complicated animal, and we can play around with how we use it and how we choose to interpret it.

The word *demon* is not inherently evil, just as the word *angel* is not inherently good. We all have different relationships with the beings around us, and the same goes for entities and spirits. A spirit who seems to bring ill will and bad luck to one person could be bringing prosperity to another. We can't really say for sure.

I choose to use the word *spirit* whenever possible to represent anyone and anything that might be conjured by a magician or a witch. Spirits are ancestors, familiars, demons, angels, gods, Akashic masters, loved ones in the beyond, and whoever else might be existing in and outside of our plane. The word *spirit* is free of moral classification, allowing us to have some freedom in how we choose to interpret our own experiences. You might choose to use your own word, or use *daimon* or *daemon*. You have that freedom and flexibility within your own journey.

ON THE ETHICS OF MAGIC

In this time and place in human history, the discussion of ethics within the context of magic and witchcraft is paramount. It's important to discuss ethics at the start of this book because of some of the content and ideas we'll be exploring.

I consider myself to be an ethical person. Still, I do accept and acknowledge that decisions or actions that seem ethical to me may not seem ethical to another, depending on that individual's perspective. Nothing we do on this plane is without consequence. A direct and seemingly positive action may actually have negative and unethical consequences or repercussions. We can't really know, and we can't spend our lives questioning the outcomes or consequences of every action.

I'm a witch, but I don't subscribe to the Threefold Law (also known as the Law of Threefold Return or Rule of Three). In most witchcraft circles, if you bring up the topic of hexing or cursing, you'll encounter someone who warns you against it, because of the Threefold Law, as if it were a millenia-old set-in-stone truth. The reality is, this law only really came about in the 1940s, when Gerald Gardner wrote his book *High Magic's Aid*, a novel about witches in medieval England, which later became incorporated into Wicca.

I'm of the belief that the Threefold Law and similar warnings in witchcraft are less concerned with the individual's safety and well-being than with controlling the individual. The threat of the Threefold Law is like the threat of hell in Christianity: it's not really grounded in anything concrete, but it does function as a means to prevent followers and disciples from straying from the path or considering their own power too heavily. Fear is a powerful method of control. People in power—including politicians, church leaders, and coven high priests—tend to be reluctant to relinquish their power once they have it.

No matter what you do in magic, there might be a consequence. But I don't think that should prevent you from doing what you need in order to protect yourself and gain access to your needs and desires. If the world were a more balanced place, there would be more cause for concern—but our world isn't especially balanced. Billionaires steal money and capitalize on the sweat and blood of their underpaid workers, and are never punished, but an impoverished mother trying to feed her baby could go to prison for stealing formula. We are allowed to believe in our own power and right to survival. We have the individual agency to do what we need in order to succeed.

The old rede is "Do what thou wilt, but harm none."

I think the more modern "Harm none, but take no shit," which circulates on the internet, is more astute.

We shouldn't set out to be violent or harm others. I don't believe in violence. I'm a vegan and a pacifist. But if someone is harassing or hurting you, a friend, or a loved one, or is doing harm to the world, I don't think the gods or the Aether is against our choosing to take matters into our own hands. After all, is it immoral to use self-defense?

Protests against racism are protection spells.

Signing a petition to maintain safe access to abortion is a protection spell.

Hexing people in power is a protection spell.

Make sigils to protect yourself, and make sigils to hex people. Magic is gray and exists on and around a spectrum. The so-called rules set in place and advisories against certain types of magic or spellwork are just more obstructions set in place to control us. You have power over your body, your own mind, and your whole being. People aim to control witches and magicians because they are afraid of our power. Those witches of yore who set these rules in place did so because they knew and were afraid of the power that we can wield, if we only grab hold of it.

Do what thou wilt. Harm none, but take no shit.

INTRODUCTION

Welcome, dear seeker, witch, artist, or whoever you are. You have opened this book, and you're preparing for a journey into the occult, the creative, the magical.

This book exists because I made sigils to help me bring a book into existence.

Let me tell you right now—magic is real. Open yourself up, and trust the mystery. Consider this book to be an invitation to begin an experiment, or to deepen an experiment you've already begun. Embrace this book as a part of your journey. Approach this book with an open mind, a sense of curiosity, and maybe even a bit of excitement.

That said, I don't want you to think that this is just a book on magic. I don't want you to think that you're about to be indoctrinated into some type of weird multilevel marketing scheme or some kind of cult. You're not. You're safe. When I say that you should approach this book with a certain level of open-mindedness and a sense of curiosity, I don't mean that you should abandon who you are or what you've carried with you to this point. Just be willing to try. Try the exercises in this book. Try making something magical. Because . . . why not? Life is nothing without experimentation.

Part of what I like about sigils is the invitation to experiment and to create. We live in a world where we're not generally invited to experiment, play, or create just for the sake of making something. Sigil crafting is not only a magical means to an end; it's also a method to connect with ourselves in deep and meaningful ways. Sigils allow us to scribble, to dream, to masturbate, to write, to do any number of things that "normal" society tells us not to do.

Sigils are a type of magic that focuses on you, your needs, and what you can bring into this world. Sigils don't ask you to buy any special stones or candles or exotic herbs. You can always add those things, but sigils just ask you to write and draw. Sigils just ask us to connect to ourselves, to open up to the Aether and the cosmos.

Sigils are a radical form of magic making.

Sigils are a radical form of spell casting.

You hold this book for a reason. Maybe you picked it up in a local bookstore while feeling lost or uncertain. Maybe you were scrolling online and you stumbled across the cover, and it spoke to you. Maybe you found it in your library's metaphysical section. Maybe you were gifted it by a friend because it made them think of you.

This book found its way to you because you have talents, needs, wants, and a sense of curiosity that isn't being met by other sources of information.

Sigil Craft is not a love-and-light kind of book. Sigil Craft isn't a book of "100 easy spells for beginners." There's nothing wrong with those kinds of books; easily consumed texts serve a purpose and help a lot of people. However, this book is not that. *Sigil Craft* is going to go a lot deeper. Why? You deserve answers. You deserve honesty. You deserve to be reminded that you have the autonomy to make choices, research on your own, and get answers.

This book won't just be teaching you how to make sigils. *Sigil Craft* is going to take you deep into the history of sigils, the application of sigils, and the places where sigils exist in the world. *Sigil Craft* is going to teach you how to make sigils, of course, but it's also going to teach you why. Why should you make sigils? Why do we make sigils the way we do? Why do certain methods work so well?

Because of the depth we'll be covering, we will be venturing into some uncomfortable topics and imagery, including some discussions around white supremacy and the alt-right. We will talk about sex and masturbation. We will talk about corporations and their logos. We're going to talk about a lot of stuff that doesn't make its way into a lot of witchcraft books.

Following is a sigil. This sigil is created to help you get the most out of this book. Let's start with a moment of play and curiosity. You're going to charge this sigil.

Look closely at the sigil. Concentrate on the shapes and the lines.

Close your eyes while holding the image of the sigil in your mind.

Think about what you want to get out of this book. Envision the sigil peeling off the page and wrapping itself around you. Envision the sigil sinking into your skin or evaporating into the air. You can breathe in the sigil and all of its power.

Take a deep breath. Breathe in all of what this sigil and this book have to offer you. Take a full, deep, chest-filling breath.

Then exhale.

Open your eyes.

What you do next is up to you, and there are no wrong answers. How do you want to engage with the sigil at this very moment? How can you make it come to life for you? How do you wish to charge this sigil to fully embody its magic? Do it.

Now, let's dig in.

NINETY-NINE THINGS THAT CAN BE LOOKED AT AS SIGILS (OR ABSOLUTELY ARE SIGILS)

1. Islamic talismanic charts
2. The written name of God in Islam
3. Tuareg talismanic jewelry
4. Signet rings
5. Mascots
6. Mandalas
7. Hobo signs
8. Tattoos
9. Tetragrammaton
10. Pennsylvania Dutch hex signs
11. Peace signs
12. Hate symbols
13. Alfred E. Neuman / "What, Me Worry?" kid
14. Popular slang
15. Star of David
16. Demonic enns
17. Chaos symbol
18. Witch bottles
19. Constellations
20. Names
21. Bujeok 부적, 符籍
22. Ofuda お札, 御札 (also known as gofu)
23. Eye of Providence
24. Heraldry, coats of arms
25. Flags (national, pride, etc.)
26. Art
27. Films of Alejandro Jodorowsky
28. Unicursal hexagram (symbol of Thelema)
29. Crosses, crucifixes
30. Aum/om, and other mantras
31. Eye of Horus
32. Ankh
33. Brand logos
34. Sacred heart
35. Rod of Asclepius (including Star of Life)
36. Caduceus
37. Jack-o'-lanterns
38. Numbers (especially when numerology is involved)
39. Written language
40. Hieroglyphs
41. Street art/graffiti (think Banksy)
42. Bowl of Hygieia
43. Tree of Life (Kabbalah)
44. Tarot cards, oracle cards
45. Signs (traffic signs, etc.)
46. Symbols created for movies, comic books, board games
47. Books
48. Political symbols
49. Representations of animals, use of animals as symbols

Chapter 1

THE HISTORY OF SIGILS

What is magic? Before we dig any deeper into what a sigil is, let's look at what magic is. The term *magic* gets tossed around all areas of the cosmic and mundane world, and in some ways, the word can start to feel a bit meaningless. Magic has become synonymous with a lot of ideas, running the gamut from charlatans to stage tricks to hyperfemininity in the form of frilly tutus and glittery wands. There's nothing wrong with those things. I love a good magic trick, and I'm all about the Disneyfied magic that exists in the world. It's fun. It's just not *magic*.

It's important to redefine magic for ourselves as witches and magicians and magical practitioners. How do you define magic for yourself, and how does magic manifest itself in your life? In *The New Tarot Handbook*, Rachel Pollack creates a spread for each card in the Major Arcana. Her spread for the Magician has some excellent questions that we can ask ourselves, whether you pull tarot cards to answer these questions or answer them through deep reflection and journaling.

1. What does magic mean to me?
2. How does magic act in my life?
3. Where do I look for it?

4. How do I find it?

5. How do I use it?

Odds are, your personal definition of magic doesn't align with what you've been told magic is, at least in terms of pop culture and mainstream media. Maybe your own personal definition surprises you, revealing that what you've learned through books and teachers isn't actually what you believe.

Magic is expansive, multicultural, old, and visceral. Humans try to put a timeline on magic and estimate how long the craft has existed in our world because we love quantification. But there is no timeline, because magic is as old as we are. Magic is timeless.

In this book, we're exploring sigils. Sigil magic is one branch of many types of magic, not even scratching the surface of what magic is and what it can be. Sigil magic, like most forms of magic, overlaps and intersects with different histories, traditions, methods, and ideas.

Most of the magic we'll be exploring in this book is sympathetic magic, a term coined by James George Frazer in the book *The Golden Bough*. Sympathetic magic is based on the principle that like attracts like. The idea breaks down further into imitative magic and contagious magic. Imitative magic relies on using two items that are similar in order to manipulate an outcome or person. This type of magic often uses correspondences, which is why we assign certain "identities" to crystals, herbs, and other magical ingredients. Whenever we make a spell jar with rose quartz for love and pink salt, we're performing imitative magic. Contagious magic is based on the idea that one thing can influence another, based on the relationship or resemblance. The clearest and most direct example of this is someone making an effigy, poppet, or voodoo doll. The outcome isn't inherently negative, but popular culture certainly makes us think so, which is why a lot of people are wary of their hair or nail clippings being collected (though in some magic, all you need is a name).

Obviously, any definition of magic is going to be a little too constricting, as it's ever shifting and ever expanding. However, understanding these principles can be helpful, especially since they can help us understand and contextualize our magic. It can also help us define whether something is or isn't a certain type of magic. A sigil can be viewed as sympathetic magic and created with that intention. But contagious magic always has room for sigils, and some sigils are examples of contagious magic. The application of these principles can drastically change how we look at sigils and how we apply them in our craft.

I'm not interested in dichotomies in magic. I'm interested in understanding context and history, and how I can apply them, without continuing to uphold older traditions of magic that don't serve me or others. Dichotomous (or binary) thinking can be extremely limiting and can leave lasting marks on our day-to-day life. The most common dichotomy that exists in magic is black versus white magic, which defines black magic as evil or malicious magic, and white magic as good or benevolent. If we let this idea persist in our own craft, we continue to perpetuate systemic and overt racism in our mundane lives, which also affects our magic. Black does not mean bad, and white does not mean good. Black magic versus white magic, high magic versus low magic, all have origins that are inherently harmful and stigmatize a lot of nonwhite forms of folk magic traditions. All magic is gray, rainbow, amorphous, and mysterious. Magic is accessible, for everyone, and universal.

WHAT IS A SIGIL?

The word *sigil* has become a lot more common in the past few years, and more and more people are using sigils in their craft. But what are they?

Sigils are symbols used in magic. That's basically it! In *The Witches' Bible*, Janet and Stewart Farrar define a sigil as "an occult seal or sign," making the careful note that the word is pronounced to rhyme with *vigil* (in case you were wondering).

Historically, sigils were a type of seal, acting as a visual representation of the name of a deity or spirit. A sigil can still be used for this purpose, but over time the idea of a sigil has evolved. A sigil can be anything visual that represents a particular purpose or intention. Some sigils start off as just symbols but become magical over time, sigilizing them through use and intention. *Magical* isn't a term inherently free of negative connotation. When I say *magical*, I mean something so full of energy and power that it is more than. Symbols can become supernatural in the power they carry. This is an idea we'll be talking about a lot later on.

It could be argued that any spell or anything symbolic can be or is a sigil. Sigils, as with art as a whole, can be incredibly subjective, and their interpretation is up to the goals and views of the artist or creator as well as the person who is observing or using them. Obviously, this can make things a bit complicated, because at what point do we stop defining something as a sigil? Can the word *sigil* lose meaning if the term is too broad? Some people will use the term *sigil* in place of the word *spell*. I'm not going to be quite this broad in its definition, but we will explore it a bit later on. In this book, a sigil is a symbol that is charged with energetic or spiritual power, or intention. For the most part, these will be two-dimensional visual objects, such as glyphs, artwork, seals, and so on. However, sigils can (and do) expand beyond this. In his book *Liber Null & Psychonaut*, Peter J. Carroll suggests that a sigil can be a pictorial glyph, a wax image, characters in a magical alphabet, or images in the mind's eye (psychic pictures). Sigils can be as simple or as complex as we wish. A sigil can be a simple stave or arcane symbol, or it can be a whole comic book or movie. Yes, you read that correctly.

Sigils become real through ancient arts and modern technology. Symbols become sigilized through human energy, intervention, and charged emotions. Sigils are emotional, volatile, radical, and integrated into our everyday life.

If we look at sigils as magical symbols, then they have existed in our world for thousands of years. Most (if not all) cultures have some kind of sigil. If you look at cultures from around the world, you'll find that they all have some kind of sigil "library"—magical symbols that are ubiquitous within that culture, or at very least common within their folk magic.

Sigils are varied and vast. Outside of utilizing them in our own magic, these magical marks can tell us a lot about a culture or a person. If we look at the creation of magical objects and markings from an anthropological and historical perspective, we can start to suss out what was important at that time and in that place. These observations can help us reflect on our own magic in new and interesting ways, allowing us to grow and evolve our craft.

Historically speaking, a lot of magical markings are connected to protection, both from malevolent entities like witches and spirits and from very real threats like disease or climate. The magic we practice and the magic that our ancestors practiced are closely knit to our fears and our dreams. While our ancestors were utilizing magical markings that helped them hunt, grow a healthy crop, or have a successful childbirth, we cast spells and make sigils that help us in sociopolitical and socioeconomic ways, as well as in tackling common concerns like getting money, calming anxiety, or manifesting an ideal job. Objectively, the inspiration for the magic looks very different, but ultimately they all boil down to the same things: safety, security, and health.

A lot of magic confronts our most human and primal fears, which means that we can learn a lot from our ancestors in terms of the magic that we can craft. While our ancestors were making a sigil for a successful hunt, we can toy with the idea of utilizing that magic for success in our own modern hunts: for a new job, a new home, or anything that satisfies the goal of offering us nourishment and shelter. Our world is very different from that of our ancestors, even from a few centuries ago, but the goal for magic is not dissimilar when we get right down to the root of it all.

The adage "those who don't learn from history are doomed to repeat it" applies to magic. While our world looks very different and our goals are varied, our primal needs and desires are still the same as our ancestors'. We have evolved, and our magic has, too. But if we learn from the magic of the world and our ancestors, we can start to learn what works and realize that some symbols and ideas might be prevalent across generations and cultures for a reason. Magic has always existed for a reason. Sigils have always existed for a reason.

In this section of the book, we'll be exploring sigils from around the world. The world is vast, and it's important to remember that magical knowledge extends beyond Westernized/European experience. Our world is ancient, and the magic of different cultures becomes intertwined through borrowing, studying, appropriating, and conquering. My approach is anthropological. While I am teaching you about these symbols and how they relate to our modern understanding of sigils, I do not claim ownership of any of them that are not part of my own culture (I call myself a European Heinz 57). Just because we discuss something in this book, that doesn't necessarily give you the license to go out and use it.

As you read this section, you may notice a lot of similarities in what these sigils are meant to accomplish and maybe even in how they look. You will also encounter ways that historical marks and art can inspire you in your own magical practice.

PENTAGRAMS AND PENTACLES

Pentagrams and pentacles are pretty common symbols in magic, witchcraft, and sigil making. Simply put, a pentagram is a five-pointed star shape made of interconnecting lines. A pentacle is that same star shape enclosed in a circle. All pentacles are pentagrams, but not all pentagrams are pentacles.

The pentagram has been found in archaeological records dating back thousands of years, appearing everywhere from Sumerian pottery to ancient Greece to early Christianity. The symbol itself dates back to at least 3500 BCE. There are even records of the pentagram being used in apotropaic magic in Europe.

The idea of the pentacle has been around almost as long, but the true pentacle really became known for magical properties with books like *The Lesser Key of Solomon*, which was compiled in the mid-seventeenth century. Eventually, the pentacle (often referred to as a pentagram) was popularized within the world of spellwork, magical practice, and ritual by Wicca in the 1960s. Since then, the pentacle has become ubiquitous within magic and witchcraft.

PENTAGRAM

PENTACLE

VEVES

Veves are sacred symbols in Vodou, used in rituals and ceremonies to represent a specific lwa (also spelled *loa*). Lwa refers to the spirits of Vodou that interact with humans and our world. Different lwa have different correspondences and can be called upon to help humans, using their individual symbols as a beacon. Veves are drawn using substances like cornmeal, wheat flour, red brick powder, gunpowder, and other materials, depending on the rite. It is said that the more accurately drawn a veve is, the more powerful it will be. One goal of an initiate is to be able to accurately draw a lwa's veve. Like many sigils that allow us to connect with spirits and deities, veves can be used in ritual or ceremony, but some practitioners will incorporate veves into an altar or even into artwork.

Because each lwa has its own veve (and because of regional differences, some lwa may have a number of veves), veves are vast and varied in appearance and design. Interestingly, some contemporary magicians have noticed similarities between veves and sigils found in the *Ars Goetia* (one of the books that make up *The Lesser Key of Solomon*). Whether there is a deeper link is unknown, and the topic hasn't really been explored. Veves are still used extensively in Vodou rituals and practices, whereas Goetic sigils tend to get used more for aesthetics or in pop culture. Such comparisons can also be dangerous, as they could lead to conflating lwa with demons, which isn't an accurate representation of lwa.

Names of Lwa

Erzulie: Goddess lwa of love, romance, beauty, and womanhood. Connected to femininity, and sometimes considered a Triple Goddess.

Maman Brigitte: Death lwa, consort of Baron Samedi. Associated with death and cemeteries, but also fertility and motherhood.

Damballah: One of the most important lwa of Vodou, traditionally represented as a giant white serpent. Said to be the primordial creator of all life.

Baron Samedi: Master of the dead, but can also give life if he sees fit. Usually found at the crossroads of the realms of the living and the dead.

JOHN DEE AND SIGILS

John Dee (1527–1608/09) was an English occultist and scientist. He was a polymath, studying and practicing in a number of fields, including mathematics, astrology, astronomy, divination, and alchemy. Dee was court astronomer and adviser to Elizabeth I, although he eventually left her service to focus on his goals of communicating with angels. He started seeking knowledge through supernatural avenues in the 1580s, eventually meeting Edward Kelley in 1582. Dee had tried the skills of a couple of mediums, but Kelley impressed him the most with his ability to scry using mirrors or crystals. It's not entirely clear why Dee decided to open up channels of communication with angelic beings to gain the knowledge he constantly sought, but this ongoing experiment (and angelic conversation) would shape a lot of occultic beliefs and ideas in future generations. It was through these channeled conversations that Dee was directed to work with a particular seal, the Sigillum Dei (Seal of God).

The Sigillum Dei was by no means an original seal that Dee created, but it was found in a grimoire that Dee likely owned, the *Liber Juratus* (also known as the *Sworn Book of Honorius*). This sigil also makes an appearance in the Italian manuscript of the *Clavicula Salomonis* (*Key of Solomon*), another infamous grimoire that John Dee likely would have been aware of, given his extensive library and status as a bona fide bibliophile. The Sigillum Dei is a complex sigil, made up of circles, a pentagram, heptagons, and a heptagram, labeled with the names of god and angels. The Sigillum Dei allegedly allows an initiated magician to have power over all creatures, with the exception of the archangels— pretty intense powers.

Through a session channeled by Kelley, Dee was instructed to carve the sigil into wax seals. The seal that John Dee carved was his version of the Sigillum Dei, known as the Sigillum Dei Aemeth (the Seal of Truth, or the Seal of God's Truth), which added more lines and detail to the existing sigil.

Dee understood that the Seal of Truth was supposed to act as a kind of filter, allowing for clearer messages to come through the channels opened by Kelley's mediumship. Think of the Sigillum Dei Aemeth as a tool that automatically cuts out unwanted static, like tuning a car radio. The idea was to cut out any unnecessary, unrelated, or deceptive information, in order to receive from the angels only messages that were actually helpful.

Prior to his work with angels, Dee worked a lot with mathematical and Hermetic ideas. It was through these studies that he created his sigil of mystical cosmic energy, the Monas Hieroglyphica, also known as the Hieroglyphic Monad. In 1564, Dee published a book that detailed the creation of his glyph, including the components and how they were pieced together to form the Monas Hieroglyphica. In this book, he details only the literal and factual aspects of the sigil, failing to (or intentionally choosing not to) explain the philosophy behind it. It is made up of symbols that represent all of the known planets at the time, arranged in a very specific and intentional way.

While it might be frustrating to not know the magical or alchemical theory behind the Monas Hieroglyphica, that alone makes it more sigilic. Dee set out to create a symbol that would represent his vision of the cosmos in unity, and he succeeded. We may want to know more, but a key part of working with a sigil is forgetting the literal meaning and the literal components that were involved in its creation.

The Monas Hieroglyphica is a fascinating sigil, which went on to be used by other alchemists and esoteric practitioners. It is found in the Rosicrucian manifesto, *The Chymical Wedding of Christian Rosenkreutz*, on a page about the main character receiving a wedding invitation (apparently an allusion to the "Sacred Marriage," which is the goal in alchemy). The appearance of the Monas Hieroglyphica in this text is part of the reason why some believe that Dee had a hand in the creation of the Rosicrucians.

John Winthrop Jr., the first governor of Connecticut and a practicing alchemist, used the Monas Hieroglyphica as an accent to his signature. Winthrop had an impressive personal library, which included a number of esoteric and occult texts. Based on a note from 1640, Winthrop held Dee's work in high esteem; he mentions the Monas Hieroglyphica specifically. Winthrop, and maybe others inspired by Dee's work, was likely motivated to use the Monas Hieroglyphica

Portrait of John Dee, featuring
his Monas Hieroglyphica

because it represents something mystical and a chapter in the pursuit of knowledge—a pursuit in which all occult and esoteric practitioners partake.

YANTRA

A yantra is a diagram or symbol, usually used for its mystical powers. Yantras are often used in the worship of deities, as meditation tools, and for the benefits they're meant to endow, such as protection, development of powers, attracting wealth or success, and so on.

Yantras mainly come from the Tantra traditions of Indian religions, such as Buddhism and Hinduism. The Indian yantras are ornate geometric designs. They are often made up of shapes like lotus leaves, triangles, and interlocking shapes. The oldest yantra known is thought to be the Sri Yantra (the most famous and ubiquitous of all yantras), which dates back to 10,000 years BCE (give or take a few thousand years). Yet, many scholars believe the oldest yantra may in fact be the Baghor stone, which dates back to at least 20,000 BCE. The Baghor stone is thought to be a site of worship and has some notable similarities to yantra like the Kali Yantra and Muladhara Chakra.

Some have theorized that Indian yantras were derived through sound patterns, like those illustrated in Ernst Chladni's book *Entdeckungen uber die Theorie des Klanges* (1787), which were produced when a plate covered in a fine powder was vibrated with a violin bow. Nowadays you can see this kind of thing in a lot of online videos, where someone places sand on or near a speaker. There is a striking similarity between the yantras and sound patterns, but we can't deny the fact that yantras have more in common with sacred geometry. The ornate interlocking shapes and lines form to create something that is truly divine.

In Southeast Asia, many Buddhist devotees get yantra tattoos, with the intention that the yantra will bestow magic and powers unto the bearer. These

Sri Yantra

KALI YANTRA

Unalome

tattoos originated with indigenous tribal beliefs but became closely connected to the idea of Hindu-Buddhist yantra. It is worth noting that nowadays a lot of people do get yantra tattoos for aesthetic reasons and little else, but there are still festivals at temples where devotees get new yantra tattoos or get their existing tattoos touched up to re-empower them.

MAGIC SQUARES

Magic squares have been used within the context of magic for almost as long as they've been used as mathematical puzzles. Concepts around magic squares even appear in the *I Ching*. While many magic squares use numbers, others utilize letters and symbols within a similar gridlike structure. Even John Dee recorded ideas like this. The most famous is likely the Sator square, a two-dimensional word square containing a five-word Latin palindrome. The oldest known example is from Pompeii, so it has pre-Christian origins. In magic, the Sator square has

been used to put out fires, remove jinxes and fevers, protect cattle from witchcraft, and guard against fatigue when traveling.

Other examples are the mystic diagrams provided by the Tamil almanacs. These magic squares, including the Sri Rama Chakra, Seetha Chakra, and others, are astrological instruments used for predicting one's future. Even the style of birth charts (Jathagam Kattam) of Tamil astrology are squares divided into grids.

ABRACADABRA

The first occurrence of the incantation *abracadabra* is in the second-century works of Serenus Sammonicus. It may originate from *Abrak*, an Egyptian word of unknown meaning. It was used for healing and protection against sickness and was prescribed like medicine by doctors.

DEMONIC AND ANGELIC SEALS

One of the most famous grimoires, *The Lesser Key of Solomon*, is a series of five books compiled in the sixteenth and seventeenth centuries. One of the books, the *Ars Goetia*, features the names and sigils of demons, as well as a brief description of each of the demons and their ranks in hell. One might use these sigils to call on these demons for a number of reasons, depending on what powers the demons embody. It is important to be mindful and use caution when considering conjuring entities like Goetic demons.

Demonic sigils and seals are a lot more common and well known, largely in part due to their use in pop culture and media, but angels also have sigils and seals. There is a bit more variation when it comes to angelic seals, with a number of grimoires offering different sigils for the same angels and archangels. Angels also have their own language, Enochian, which was channeled and conceptualized by John Dee in the sixteenth century.

The most well-known demonic seal (which could also be considered an angelic seal, depending on your point of view) is likely the Sigil of Lucifer. Lucifer was one of god's angels but fell from heaven because of his sin of self-deification. The mythology and story of Lucifer varies, but the through line is that Lucifer is a fallen angel. Lucifer has two symbols, one of which is also the alchemical symbol for sulfur. Symbols relating to Lucifer are generally used within satanic or Luciferian paths.

Goetic Demons

Bael: Also known as Ball. King of hell and head of the infernal powers, according to the *Ars Goetia*. Commands sixty-six legions of demons, and has three heads: a toad, a man, and a cat.

Bathin: Duke of hell. Commands thirty legions of demons. Knows the virtues of precious stones and herbs, and helps one attain astral projection. Can bring humans suddenly from one place to another and can take you where you need to go.

Barbas: Great president of hell, who truthfully answers questions on hidden or secret things. Can cause or heal disease, teaches mechanical arts, and can transform humans into other shapes.

Sigil of Lucifer

LATVIAN STAVES

When I started making sigils, I struggled. I had initially tried learning the magic-squares method of sigil crafting, and it did not click with me. Not long after in my magical journey, I discovered the style of sigil crafting that I would learn was created by Austin Osman Spare. I was researching the folk magic and magical practices of my ancestors. I'm a combination of all types of European: Scottish, British, Baltic German/Latvian, French, Irish, Welsh, Prussian/Russian. My maternal grandfather was born in Riga, Latvia, and I felt called to learn about that part of my heritage. In my studies and research, I discovered Latvian staves, and I was surprised by what I saw. The types of sigils that I crafted shared striking similarities with the magical marks my ancestors made.

Magical folk symbols like Latvian staves might persist in the Baltic region because the area was one of the last parts of Europe to be Christianized; some parts remained pagan until the fifteenth century. The staves are connected to the region's mythology and folk beliefs and are usually used to represent deities. The symbols are runic, geometric shapes, often consisting of straight lines. To this day, the symbols continue to make appearances in folk art, offering protection and other powers from the corresponding deity. One benefit to using simple symbols that are made up of straight lines is that they're easily replicated through carving, metalwork, and the creation of textiles, including weaving.

I think about the idea of genetic memory a lot; there are certain things we are predisposed to just by being human, like creating and using language. I also think about ancestral memory. In the scope of witchcraft, the idea of ancestral curses or ancestral trauma comes up, which focuses on the negative things that have happened to and shaped your ancestral line and continue to exist in you. This ancestral pain calls for healing. Conversely, and coexisting with the pain, is ancestral knowledge, which you can learn from and use. You are a combination of all of your ancestors, and they live on through your DNA, your thoughts, and your ideas. You might be surprised to see that you're naturally tapping into your ancestral knowledge. You can also explore how your ancestors would incorporate symbols into their day-to-day life and ritual practices. You may be inspired to learn similar practices in order to charge and bring your sigils to life.

Ancestral knowledge is always within us, but sometimes it's difficult to access. Recent trauma, colonization, Christianization, being adopted, and a million other things can make it so that it's a lot harder to feel or understand the ancestral knowledge that we hold. If this is the case for you, you can experiment with how you touch base with your ancestors and learn from them directly. You might talk to them, meditate with them, or open yourself up for channeling. Perhaps you're interested in accessing the Akashic records (a compendium of everything to have ever occurred on the planet, in the past, present, and future), which would be an excellent avenue for this kind of exploration. You can do research based on what you know, and see what comes through when you incorporate cultural practices from your ancestry. Ancestral knowledge doesn't even need to come from blood. Ancestral knowledge exists in what we learn from those near us. You can experiment based on what you know and based on the family who raised you (and that includes chosen family).

Some Latvian Staves

The Cross of the Moon: Related to agriculture and is a sign of growth and disasters. Also a symbol of protection for soldiers. The moon is seen as a paternal figure in Latvian folklore.

Mara's Earth: Symbol of the material world. Mara is the defender of women and ruler of both earth and underground. Mara is a goddess-mother. The Mother of Earth protects the dead, and Mara is the ruler of other goddesses, such as Wind, Sea, and Milk. I included this symbol because it illustrates how a magical symbol does not need to be overly complex.

Saule: The sun, representing health, harmony, light, and eternity and its endlessness. Saule is also a protective force.

Mara's Cross: Representation of fertility, completeness, fire, and the home. Often found on fresh-baked pies and fireplaces. A symbol of protection for women.

Clockwise from top left:
Cross of the Moon,
Mara's Earth, Saule,
Mara's Cross

Exploring Sigils from Your Ancestry and Your Family History

Examine your family history, your culture, or any part of your ancestry and look for symbols. Don't worry too much about what they mean. For this exercise, just look at the symbols. Consider the symbols that really jump out to you: What do they look like? What do they have in common? How do they make you feel?

You can do this same exercise with other symbols from around the world. You can even do this with icons or modern symbols.

ADINKRA SYMBOLS

Adinkra symbols are visual symbols, usually fairly graphic and simple in appearance, but rich with historical and philosophical significance. These symbols originated with the Gyaman people of Ghana and Côte d'Ivoire, originally printed on cloth worn by royals and meant to be worn to important ceremonies. Over time, Adinkra symbols have become globally important; they are now found in all kinds of artwork and places, from earthenware pots to logos for universities in Ghana. The symbols carry a certain amount of gravitas, while also communicating deep truths and philosophies.

Some of the symbols carry a certain level of recognizability, incorporating universal symbols like a heart. Others conceal and embody complex concepts and truths, which the wearer or user understands on a deep level. The symbols carry a similarity to a lot of symbols that we see around the world, but that detail is secondary to the way that the Adinkra symbols act as strong sigils.

Adinkra symbols run the gamut in meaning and purpose, and the symbols interact with one another through different combinations. Cloth is another example of a way that sigils can be incorporated into our day-to-day life. Each Adinkra cloth features all kinds of these symbols, creating something personal, magical, and purposeful. Oftentimes, the fabrics are given specific names to convey the meaning behind the cloth and why it was created. Historically, Adinkra cloth was woven, but now the cloth is created through block printing or silk-screening.

ICELANDIC MAGICAL STAVES

Galdrastafir are magical staves from Iceland (the name is a combination of the words *galdra*, meaning magical, and *stafi*, or sticks). These staves are usually runic in appearance, and some have theorized that their appearance and linework are directly related to the runic alphabets. The origins of Galdrastafir are ultimately unknown, due to a combination of oral history and destruction of early records. Most staves that we know have been recovered from grimoires, most of which are nineteenth-century compilations of information from older texts. The oldest known Icelandic grimoire is the *Galdrabók*, which was started sometime in the late sixteenth century, with additions being made until the mid-seventeenth century. This grimoire contains forty-seven spells and sigils, containing information from four different contributors.

Staves vary in purpose and intention, from protection to success in farmwork to love spells to killing others, sometimes including specific instructions and details of how to properly use the magical symbols and their power. Icelandic staves are a good example of using sigils as a component in greater spellwork, almost acting as spell ingredients in their own right.

In the past, science and magic were one and the same, and practitioners of the craft wouldn't have considered that there would ever be a difference. You practiced magic to achieve results. There is a level of experimentation, and sometimes a level of secrecy (with practitioners going so far as to write their spells in complex codes). There is a noticeable evolution in the complexity of symbols and spells, as well as the adoption and integration of different ideologies and theories, including those of mainstream Christianity after the Christianization of Iceland in 1000 CE.

Two types of magic were practiced in Iceland: galdur and seidh (seiðr). Galdur is the type of magic that accounts for most staves, as well as the content of most of the grimoires. Galdur is generally regarded as more analytical and seems to be more results-focused, not unlike modern chaos magic. Galdur utilizes rune magic, as well as vocal formulas (incantations, mantras). Seidh is a more intuitive form of magic, closely connected to Old Norse gods (Odin and Freya, in particular), and leans more toward shamanic practices that include more "natural" methods, such as incorporating animal and vegetable components. Both magicks were in existence during the "heathen period" of Iceland (ca. 870–1000) and continued to be practiced afterward. While both were accepted forms of magic, the different practices did start to take on gendered and moral connotations. Galdur was considered more "honorable," whereas seidh was viewed as a feminine practice, casting seidh into the shadows of "shameful." If a man practiced seidh, he was called seiðmaðr and generally perceived as "unmanly." While not respected, men practicing seidh were also not rare. In general, Iceland is an interesting outlier, as most practitioners of the craft were men, and when witch trials came to Iceland in the sixteenth century, most of the victims were men.

When we are creating our own sigils, we can look to the galdrastafir for inspiration in how we apply them to the world around us, how we incorporate them into larger spells, and how we can incorporate other symbols and letters.

One of the most infamous artifacts of spellwork to come out of Iceland are the nábrók, or necropants. The creation of necropants is one of the most difficult feats described in grimoires and folk tales. The goal is to create a supernatural tool that will create an endless supply of money (for generations, if done correctly). The sorcerer begins by making a pact with someone, so that you may use their skin after death. The person in question needs to be someone with a scrotum.

This is going to get weird, and gross. After the individual has died, you must dig up their body and skin the corpse, so that the skin from the waist down is in one piece (the skin must not have holes or scratches, either). When the sorcerer steps into the "pants," they will stick to the sorcerer's skin. A coin must be stolen from a poor widow on Christmas, Easter, or Whitsunday, and kept in the scrotum along with the nábrókarstafur drawn on a piece of paper. The coin will draw money into the scrotum, and it will never empty as long as the original coin is not removed. The necropants will continue to work for generations, but the sorcerer must convince another person to take ownership and step into each leg of the pants as the sorcerer steps out so the pants are always being worn by somebody. The necropants cannot function without the sigil, and this is a common thread in a lot of galdrastafir-based magic.

As we discussed earlier, the aim of most magic has been structured around goals of comfort, security, success, or protection. This goal really hasn't changed, and through this understanding, we can look to past sigils and observe how we might use preexisting magic to our own advantage.

How can we utilize ancient sigils for our modern purposes? How can we use livestock staves or sigils? Or those for finance? How can we look to centuries-old sigils for inspiration?

Later on, we will explore distilling desires or goals down to the simplest and most direct terms. If we distill our desires down to their root, we can start to look at new ways to approach them magically. Simplifying our terminology and goals can sometimes mean that we open up new options for how we achieve magical goals. An Icelandic stave for protecting livestock can be used to protect our household animals or pets. We can use those sigils to protect animals being abused by factory farms. A sigil for "something unclean" can be drawn on hand sanitizer or antibiotics to help us get healthy faster.

We can even charge these older symbols to better suit our own needs. Magic is all about evolution and adaptation, and there's nothing stopping us from approaching ancient markings in new ways, especially since that's a component in how those old markings were created.

Some Icelandic Staves

Helm of Awe: A fear inducer and a source of protection. There are variations, including some that have become very common with the realms of neo-Paganism and witchcraft. The specific powers it holds vary slightly depending on how it's drawn, but the bottom line is that it's always some kind of protective mark. Originally, it was to be carved in lead and pressed on one's forehead. This symbol is mentioned in Eddic poetry and is also known as Aegishjalmur.

If Something Unclean Is Around: An example of a simpler stave or sigil. This is a protective symbol against something unclean (unwanted, negative, and so on). The symbol should be carved on the doorframe over the entrance to a house, using an awl made of juniper or silver.

Helm of Awe

If something
unclean is around

APOTROPAIC MAGIC

Apotropaic magic, protection against evil, has been around for a really long time, and a lot of its symbols and concepts appear in modern witchcraft. Interestingly, a lot of apotropaic pieces of magic (sigils, talismans, or what have you) were used to defend against witches. Witches were often seen on the same level as demons or evil spirits and were worth protecting your home from.

Apotropaic magic is one of the oldest forms of magic. Because it's so old, a lot of these types of magic end up being used by modern witches, despite the fact that historically, these witches would have been grouped with evils worth defending against. For the longest time, you were often condemned if you practiced any type of magic, but an exception to that was if you practiced apotropaic magic or any type of magic that helped you find witches.

Magic evolves with us. Magic evolves with our needs and wants, and through the reclamation of power. Because of this, symbols and methods and meanings evolve, too. The original DNA is usually maintained, but the correspondences and uses change with the times. What started off as being used to defend against evil or witches or devils is now used as a tool against negative or unwanted energy. We see this in the way we discuss spell ingredients, but we also see it in the symbols that we use.

One example is the "devil's horns" hand gesture. Ronnie James Dio popularized this hand gesture because allegedly he didn't want to do a peace sign like

Ozzy Osbourne. Dio's widow Wendy Dio explained that he did it because his grandmother would do the sign. It's an old Italian sign called malocchio (the evil eye), used to ward off evil. However, Geezer Butler (bassist of Black Sabbath) said that he did the hand gesture because he saw images of occultist Aleister Crowley doing it and he showed the symbol to Dio. Even before Dio took over as the lead singer of Black Sabbath, other musicians have been photographed making similar hand gestures, including John Lennon and members of the band Coven.

Regardless of who popularized it, the hand signal has taken on new meaning. While this gesture likely did start off as a way to protect against the evil eye, we can't deny that most of us relate it to rock and roll and that plenty of conspiracy theories accuse politicians and celebrities of being devil worshippers because they have been seen making the sign—though, more often than not, they are actually making the American Sign Language symbol for "I love you," a similar-looking yet distinct symbol.

The concern around magic and malevolent things comes from a real place. Vermin like rats can enter homes via openings so small that it seems like they come from nowhere. They create problems by stealing food or small items, ruining possessions, or even bringing disease and sickness. Without a reasonable explanation beyond witchcraft, individuals would resort to apotropaic magic to ward them off. In his essay "Evidence of Unseen Forces: Apotropaic Objects on the Threshold of Materiality," Brian Hoggard writes about concealed objects and marks used as protection against supernatural forces, including witchcraft and demons. When people find these objects in their homes, they'll often approach individuals like Hoggard with a strong sense of concern. As he writes, "They suddenly become aware of the presence of former occupants and feel a connection to the same fears they had." As humans, we continue to be afraid of the unknown and the unseen.

A lot of apotropaic magic, particularly in English witchcraft records, comes from the fear of witches' familiars, which could slip into spaces that witches themselves couldn't. Their familiars would deliver the spells of the witch. The belief that witches could send their familiars to do their bidding created a deep sense of vulnerability, leading people to become hyperaware of all of the problems in their homes. Chimneys, doorways, windows, and attics posed concerns. A lot of apotropaic objects like witch bottles and shoes were found around the hearth. Door and window lintels frequently bore marks of protection, and practitioners might even leave broken knife blades to ward off witches. Boggard writes of an inn in Bretforton, Worcestershire, that would whitewash all of the gaps and cracks in the building so that there were no dark spaces in which malevolent forces could hide. The same inn had three circles drawn in front of the fireplace to protect it (circles are supposedly protective because they don't have any corners in which dark forces like witches can hide).

Apotropaic marks—especially in Europe—were carved into wood or stone. For a long time, archaeologists thought that some markings were simply carpenter's marks, but the shapes are typically too ornate to be random or mundane in that way. They included sun symbols, eyes, *M* figures, triangles, hexagrams, hexafoils, or other intentionally created geometric shapes. These so-called witches' marks (not to be confused with witch marks, which we'll discuss later on) were carved to keep witches from flying into a house through openings like a window or chimney.

There are also interlocking *V* shapes, which are theorized to have been used to invoke the Virgin Mary for protection. Witches' marks like these have been found in caves and caverns all over England, including Goatchurch Cavern and Wookey Hole (which has a witch legend associated with it). The repetition of the marks eliminates them as carpenter or mason marks, but why individuals would draw them in caves (especially as recently as the sixteenth through eighteenth centuries, as the markings are approximately dated) is a question that has yet to be answered. Perhaps the intention was to confine the evil to the caves.

Aside from witches, another unseen threat was the evil eye. While it has come to be associated with witchcraft in some ways, it is actually a universal concept in which someone unknowingly (usually) curses another. The evil eye is like a destructive gaze that projects envy and ill will toward an individual. Belief in the evil eye dates back to ancient times, possibly to the ancient Ugarit (around 1250 BCE). The most common forms of apotropaic magic that persist today are defenses against the evil eye (including hamsa and nazar charms). There is even an emoji for the nazar.

Whether it's from witches or the negative energy of another person, the goal of apotropaic magic is the same: to protect the individual and their home. Apotropaic magic can exist in three-dimensional shapes, such as amulets, talismans, or even concealed objects like shoes, dried cats, horse skulls, or witch bottles. Sigils can be created with the intention of being apotropaic magic, and many symbols used in apotropaic magic become sigils through their repeated use. They may not have a literal meaning, but the intention is understood.

Chapter 2

ART AND SIGILS

When we explore art history and read manifestos from various art movements, we discover a relationship to magic that is inherent through the language. The creation of art is magic. Magic making is an art. It's not exactly arbitrary that the word *witchcraft* contains the suffix *craft*, and you cannot spell *witchcraft* without *art*. It's only practical that we use artistic techniques within our magic, and vice versa. Humans are inclined to create. Most of us have some desire to create, whether it's art, writing, cooking, or parenting. It is one of our innermost desires to conjure something into reality, to bring something forth into the material world. This way, not only can we experience it within our imagination and mind's eye, but others can experience it (in some way) in the physical world. We have a desire to create something and set it loose upon the world. That concept of the world doesn't even need to be especially expansive; the world can be our bedroom or our living room. Just because someone else doesn't see or interact with something directly doesn't mean that it doesn't exist in their world.

That goes for magic, too.

While I was researching for this book, I became deeply inspired by a lot of the words that I was reading around art and art making. My university education led to a bachelor's degree in fine art in fiber, and the art-history aspect of that education was always some of the most interesting to me. Yes, making is wonderful. But there's something so fascinating about how people write about art. Reading art essays or manifestos is not unlike reading a grimoire. Both are examples of works that offer a certain degree of how-to, but not to the point that the reader isn't doing a paint-by-numbers (or casting a spell by numbers?). The reader is encouraged to go deep, to understand, and to apply what they are reading to their own practice or craft. In turn, the individual who was once the reader—the student—may discover or develop concepts or techniques that are radical and new, which the student will then write about or share, thus transforming the student into a teacher. Art and magic are two areas of practice that encourage replication but inevitably lead to new forms of expression and ideas, which will then form their own schools of thought within the practice.

> "Perhaps the art which we are seeking is the key to every former art: a salomonic key that will open all mysteries."
>
> —Hugo Ball, April 18, 1917

Dada sparked artistic movements that questioned what art was and how art could be created. The methods through which Dada art was created are not unlike the methods through which a preexisting symbol is sigilized through intention and energy. Marcel Duchamp's "readymades" radicalized art, transmuting everyday objects into something more than ordinary. Suddenly, the inherent meaning or understanding is not the only relevant view of an object. A mundane object could suddenly become art, entirely because someone chose to see it that way and make it so.

When we are making sigils or any kind of magic, we can learn a lot from art movements like Dada. Dadaists were comfortable with abandoning what critics and the audience would view and measure in order to deem something art. This allowed for abstraction, experimentation, insertion of emotions and questions, and the continued question *what is art?*

Sigils are abstract art created through magic.

We don't need to behold ourselves to a particular style, aesthetic, or skill set. There is no measure as to what makes a sigil successful, beyond whether or not it works. If it is functional but ugly or gross, the function outweighs the aesthetics of the sigil. The sigil is successful through its ability to work, and that is it.

An Experiment: Reconceptualizing Familiar Things

Marcel Duchamp disrupted the art world when he submitted a urinal signed "R. Mutt" to an exhibition. While the exhibition committee rejected it, it was shown at Alfred Stieglitz's studio. He transmuted an ordinary object into art. Can you take a preexisting symbol or object and transmute it into a sigil for your purpose? Can you remove the original purpose or meaning from that symbol or object? What benefit do you think exists through the possibility of transmuting an ordinary object into something magical or otherworldly, into a sigil?

If we look to art, especially radical art movements that shifted perspectives, can we apply the methods to our sigils? Not just in how we physically create the sigil to bring it into the material world (through paints, chalks, sculpture, etc.), but in how we contextualize our sigil crafting? Countless art movements and periods in art changed the way that people thought about art. How can we apply similar ideas to change the way we think about magic? How can we use art to change how we create magic?

> "The work of art becomes an independent, artistically alive organism in which everything counterbalances everything else."
> —Theo van Doesburg, from *Principles of Neo-Plastic Art*

Sounds like magic, doesn't it?

PETROGLYPHS AND EARLY HUMAN ART

According to archaeologists and anthropologists, the oldest known artwork dates back to the Lower Paleolithic period, making it at least 290,000 years old (though it may be older). The oldest example is the Bhimbetka petroglyphs, found in India. The oldest markings are small, round depressions carved out of stone (called cupules). The markings may be as old as 700,000 years old, which means that they may predate *Homo sapiens*. It's pretty cool to think that the need and interest in mark making may be that old. Even 290,000 years is mind-boggling. It really speaks to human ingenuity. It starts to feel like art and creation are part of our genetic memory.

The oldest known figurative art is the Borneo cave paintings in Indonesia, thought to be around 52,000 years old. These paintings depict figures that look like cattle, showing early humans making connections between what they saw in the world and what they could create. In his essay "Pop Magic!," Grant Morrison suggests that the history of sigil magic dates back to these first drawings. While they may not be intentionally magical, paleolithic artifacts and artwork created by our ancestors are the first sigils. Early humans were creating art with a specific intent and purpose in mind. Early humans created images and objects to connect with things that were present in their lives, and maybe even to represent what they wanted. This is manifestation. This creation of art is sympathetic magic at work. The Upper Paleolithic period was the first time that pottery was used to make

figures, rather than practical tools like food storage or dishes. Our ancient ancestors were creating art, and through it they were starting to conjure their desires.

Archaeologists have recently discovered that modern humans may have been missing some vital keys in properly viewing and understanding ancient cave art. Ancient artists created these artworks in dark caves, devoid of natural light. In some caves, different parts of the drawings are rendered several times, and the light and shadows created by the light of fire may have created the illusion that the figures were moving. Instead of an eight-legged bison, the illustration is actually a running animal, intended to be viewed in a specific type of light. While research is ongoing, this idea of intentionally creating images and artwork to be viewed in a specific light can inspire us in how we create our own sigils and magical imagery.

GEOGLYPHS

Petroglyphs from around the world share a lot of similarities in their appearance, and a lot of the imagery that we see in these ancient marks is echoed in the history of art and sigils. In some instances, the shapes and symbols are formed as geoglyphs, large designs that are usually longer than four meters and created by altering the ground in some way. This can be done by carving into the earth and pushing away the topsoil to reveal a different color of earth underneath (a negative geoglyph), or by arranging items like stones on the earth (a positive glyph).

Some geoglyphs have been created by contemporary artists, but older examples exist around the world. Arguably, the most famous example is the Nazca Lines in Peru. These massive shapes were created in the Nazca Desert between 500 BCE and 500 CE. The true intention of the Nazca lines is unknown, but archaeologists have suggested that they may act as astrological or cosmological markers, or they may have been created to be seen by deities in the sky. Based on our modern worldview, it's easy to look at ancient creations and observe them as

OXFORDSHIRE · ENGLAND

NAZCA DESERT · PERU

magical. While it might not be 100 percent accurate, these perceptions can act as a jumping-off point for our own purposes. While we might not venture out to create something as massive as the Nazca Lines (and maybe we shouldn't, because we don't know what type of environmental impact land art can have), we can be inspired to carve our sigils into stones or earth. We can look to art like petroglyphs, pictographs, and geoglyphs as inspiration for how we draw our sigils, what

AUSTIN OSMAN SPARE

CAMERON

FRIDA KAHLO

ROSALEEN "ROIE" NORTON

we can turn into a sigil, and how we can interact with the outdoor world to help activate and charge our sigils.

CAMERON

Marjorie Cameron (April 23, 1922–June 24, 1995), who preferred the mononym Cameron, was an American artist, poet, actress, and witch. Her life became entwined with the occult after meeting Jack Parsons, a cofounder of the Jet Propulsion Laboratory, who believed that he conjured Cameron, his ideal woman, through a series of Thelemic sex magic rituals. When Parsons died in 1952 from an explosion, Cameron burned her early paintings and drawings in a ritual of mourning and rebirth. She would later perform blood magic rituals in an attempt to communicate with Parsons's spirit.

Peter Lunenfeld writes, "Cameron was one of those people for whom art was life, and life was art." Her work is one of many bodies of occultic art that carried sexual tones, causing concern among more conservative members of society (and leading to the arrest of at least one individual). A vast majority of her work is based on occult and metaphysical themes and ideas. A friend of Cameron's, filmmaker Kenneth Anger, once said that Cameron considered her work to be talismans. She would often destroy her work. Anger said, "If she destroyed some of them, it was for magical reasons that [she] consigned them to the flames."

Throughout her life, Cameron struggled with mental illness, and she was likely institutionalized at one time. Many around her saw her passion for the occult as dangerous, given her mental health, but she persisted in her pursuit of the metaphysical, especially through art.

Since her death, Cameron has become a kind of symbol of the quintessential Californian, because she made herself up. She is considered a Los Angeles witch icon, even after death.

AUSTIN OSMAN SPARE

Austin Osman Spare (December 30, 1886–May 15, 1956) is the reason we make sigils the way we do now. Many people use magic squares to create sigils, but most people use Spare's method because of how intuitive it is. He's also the reason that we use sigils for the tools they are.

Spare wrote, "Sigils are the art of believing; my invention for making belief organic, ergo, true belief."

Spare was an English artist and occultist. He was influenced by symbolism and Art Nouveau, and used lines to create intricate work—which also lent itself to his creation of sigils and magical writing.

Spare developed idiosyncratic magical techniques, including automatic writing, automatic drawing, and sigilization. All of these techniques are based on the relationship between the conscious and unconscious self. Spare developed his own magico-religious philosophy, which has come to be known as Zos Kia Cultus. Spare denounced Christianity when he was seventeen, stating, "I am devising a religion of my own which embodies my conception of what; we are, we were, and shall be in the future." Some of Spare's techniques, particularly sigils and the creation of an "alphabet of desire," were adopted, adapted, and popularized by Peter J. Carroll in the work *Liber Null & Psychonaut*. This led to Spare's ideas and techniques being used as a part of chaos magick.

ROSALEEN "ROIE" NORTON

Rosaleen "Roie" Norton (October 2, 1917–December 2, 1979) was an Australian artist known as the Witch of King's Cross. Norton used her art as a means to communicate with gods, demons, and other entities, which brings to mind classic sigils like Sigillum Dei and other sigils meant to evoke spirits and gods. Norton was devoted to Pan and created a number of artworks inspired by or focused on him. In the 1940s, she experimented with self-hypnosis and automatic drawing as an aspect of her work, leading to her discovery of techniques that heightened her artistic perception by transferring her conscious attention at will to inner planes of awareness.

In 1951, four of her pictures were seized by the police. She was prosecuted on the allegation that her works could "deprave and corrupt the morals of those who saw them" and that they were inspired by the works of medieval demonology. Norton's art was defended by scholars, because of the connections of Greek mythology. Still, harsh censorship was rampant due to social and political conservatism in Australia and the predominance of Christianity. Tabloids and scandals seemed to follow her, but she didn't really seem to care, and she continued to make her art and practice witchcraft.

Norton was inspired by the "night" side of magic, allegedly partaking in sex magic as well as bondage and sadomasochism. She was bisexual, queer, and free-spirited.

FRIDA KAHLO

Frida Kahlo (July 6, 1907–July 13, 1954) was born Magdalena Carmen Frieda Kahlo y Calderón, in Coyoacan, a suburb of Mexico City. She was queer and a Communist, regularly dressed in men's clothing, and embraced her Mexican heritage and culture. She is one artist who is represented more by her self-portraits than through any other method. Do these paintings accurately represent her? Or do they transform her into an icon? Is Frida Kahlo more a hypersigil than a person?

Frida Kahlo said, "I paint self-portraits because I am the person I know best. I paint my own reality. The only thing I know is that I paint because I need to and I paint whatever passes through my head without any consideration."

There is a lot of depth to the work that Frida Kahlo created. Her work is deeply connected to the traumas in her life, the most significant being the bus accident she suffered in 1925. In 1926 she painted her first self-portrait, which offered a channel for her to chart her life, allowing her to process her trauma, pain, and emotional reactions. She continued to suffer health problems, reaching the lowest point when her leg had to be amputated due to gangrene. She suffered miscarriages and weight loss, and was bedridden for months.

One art critic wrote, "Never before had a woman put such agonized poetry on canvas as Frida." She documented her life from an angle that captured the emotional and physical pain in a very real way. Death is not only a theme in her paintings but a medium alongside paint.

Creating a Hypersigil through Self-Portraiture

Create a self-portrait using symbols and iconography that represents who you wish to be. You can create this through collage, digital art, crayons, or whatever medium you like. Maybe you don't even draw your face; maybe you create something that captures the essence of who you are.

Set aside this self-portrait for about a week (or however long feels good), and return to it with fresh eyes. How do you feel about the art? How do you feel about yourself? This isn't about criticizing yourself. This is about radical self-love and radical self-acceptance.

Self-portraits can be incredibly powerful tools for creating a hypersigil—that is, creating a sigil so big that it changes reality and perception. If you looked at this self-portrait every day, how would you feel about yourself? Would you start to change your perception of yourself? Would you start to recognize new power within yourself?

SELF-PORTRAITS AS HYPERSIGILS

Most self-portraits are hypersigils to some degree. Take the self-portraits of artists from past eras who are long deceased. Our perception of these artists is created almost entirely through our interpretations of their self-portraits. While the portraits may not be accurate in terms of how the artist actually looked, these representations are often referred to more than photographs. If you think of some artists, you'll picture their work before they picture their faces. The art that an artist creates is often so closely tied to their work that the artist becomes their art. This makes it exceedingly difficult to separate the art from the artist, despite the fact that the art someone makes may have little to no bearing on who they actually are or what they believe. Sometimes art is an absolute work of fiction, but we will still use the art (especially if it's visual art like painting, drawing, or textiles) as a reference point for their identity.

There is always an aspect of storytelling within art, which affects our perception of the artist and their identity. This perception may be completely false; but if it is created by the artist, wouldn't it stand to reason that the artist had a hand in shaping that perception? Is the artist responsible for the reaction their art receives? Is the artist responsible for how we perceive them because of their art?

Self-portraits are, arguably, one of the most common forms of hypersigil, but hypersigils can be created through other methods. Sigils alter reality through intervening or changing the world through magic, but hypersigils take it to another level. The most famous example of a hypersigil is Grant Morrison's graphic novel series *The Invisibles*. Through the creation of this comic book (and hypersigil), Morrison changed their appearance, took on traits of characters within the comics, and manifested aspects of the story into reality. Morrison changed themself in radical ways, transforming into this leveled-up version of themself. This process wasn't all positive, though. When the character who resembled them most closely became sick in the comic book, Morrison themself ended up in the hospital. *The Invisibles* was some powerful magic at work.

Hypersigils also appear in our online personas. For example, trans and queer people may exist as their true selves in online spaces before coming out in "real life." This allows for a more comfortable transition, but it also gives individuals a chance to realize who their ideal self is or, rather, how to accurately represent how they feel inside. This doesn't only happen with queer people, though. Manifesting your authentic self through the internet is something we all do. It may not even make its way fully to our away-from-keyboard life, but we are at least able to carry some essence of that version of ourselves that feels more comfortable and accurate.

The persona we create online is a self-portrait. What we share online creates an essence of who we are, representing our beliefs, interests, political stances, and so on. We can also start to embody different beliefs and ideals based on who we follow. If we follow the "wrong" type of people, they can start to shape us into something else, and that will bleed into our real world. Can someone else form us into a hypersigil of their ideal being? Arguably, yes. It's toxic, and it's bad magic, but it happens.

I lived my truth as a nonbinary person openly online long before I started discussing it with anyone outside of the digital space. Even when I wasn't fully aware that I was nonbinary and kept floundering with my gender identity, unsure of what I was, my online persona still gave off nonbinary vibes to others. Was I unintentionally sigilizing my own identity, creating a hypersigil that allowed me to be more open and comfortable in my away-from-keyboard life? If it wasn't for my online persona, I don't know how I would have ever broached the topic with people in my day-to-day life. That being said, I'm still not out with a lot of my friends. To them, I'm still a cis she/her, and I doubt I'll ever bring up my identity clearly. There's something about having my online persona that allows me to be comfortable in my skin, even when it is difficult. It's like some kind of protection spell, or a suit of armor.

When I was reading different interpretations of the hypersigil, I had just pulled the 6 of Wands reversed. In my day-to-day tarot practice, I've been working with Rachel Pollack's book *The New Tarot Handbook*. It's a wonderful, magical, exquisitely written book on tarot, focusing primarily on interpretations around the Smith-Waite deck. Pollack's interpretation of the 6 of Wands reversed includes the phrase "going your own way, without need of followers." One of the most important aspects of magic is making your life more interesting, doing things that make you feel like your most magical self, and doing things for yourself (rather than doing things based on how others perceive you or how they need you to be). The hypersigil is considered one of the highest workings of magic because of this. If you can create a sigil so massive and powerful that it completely transforms you, then you're a pretty damn powerful witch.

Through all of this, I've come to the conclusion that while gendering concepts or things isn't for me, that doesn't invalidate the need or desire for others. While my hypersigils may involve making myself comfortable in my gender identity outside of a binary, another's hypersigil may help them navigate their identity within a gender binary.

Protection Spell to Fortify Your Authentic Self Online

- Black tourmaline, shungite, smoky quartz (one, or all three)
- Witch hazel
- Cleaning cloth
- Black cloth
- Salt
- A sigil for protection

Best timing for the spell: Dark moon, or whenever needed

If you are starting to feel bombarded by things online that affect who you are, take a moment to turn off your phone and cover any mirrors in your space. Phones are extremely energetic objects. They are portals. When we hold our phone, we are holding the entire world. We are holding a portal from us to other people, to the past, to the present, and to our hopes, dreams, and fears. It's . . . a lot. It's an immense amount of power, vulnerability, and technology. The TV show *Black Mirror* is named that because the screens in our life become mirrors when the screens are turned off. Even when they're turned on, the content of our phones is a mirror. So it's not a bad idea to take a break from time to time and actively turn off your phone.

When your phone is shut off, wipe it down with witch hazel on a cleaning cloth. You can find this potent liquid in the first aid section of a grocery store or drugstore. Witch hazel is protective, but it is used in first aid for a reason—it heals a lot of minor wounds like burns, insect bites, and acne. Personally, I use it as a toner for my skin. I also add it to a lot of sprays I make because the alcohol content acts as a preservative. Because of the alcohol, it also sanitizes your phone to a degree.

Wrap your phone in the black cloth, and lay the phone face (screen) down on a table where it won't be disrupted. Place the crystal(s) on the cloth, and surround the bundle with a circle of salt to fully contain the portal so you can take a break.

While you take a break, make a sigil to protect your authentic online self, using your sigil method of choice.

Once you're ready to turn to your phone, scoop up the salt and scatter it into the wind or anywhere away from your home. You can even intentionally place it in the trash (outside your house), saying something like "I remove all of the internet garbage from my space" or whatever incantation feels good.

Wash the black cloth, and cleanse your crystals.

Photograph your sigil or make it into a digital drawing. Set it as your phone's lock screen or wallpaper, or incorporate it as a secret sigil into your profile pictures. You're clever, and you know what feels best for you.

Repeat this spell as needed. The waning moon or dark moon will be best suited for this kind of magic—but, as with any magic, it's survival: you gotta do it when you gotta do it.

Chapter 3

SIGILS IN THE MODERN WORLD

Chaos magick is often called results-based magic. It focuses on the success of spells and results from magic, opting to strip away the ceremony and ornamentation present in more traditional forms of magic, such as Wicca or the Golden Dawn. Chaos magick works on the tenet that "belief is a tool for achieving effects." Chaos magick has a DIY approach, encouraging practitioners to take on their own style, methods, and practice to develop something entirely their own.

Chaos magick arose out of England in the 1970s, largely based on writings of Austin Osman Spare. The early leading figures include Peter J. Carroll and Ray Sherwin. The first use of the word *chaos* in relation to magic was by Peter J. Carroll in *Liber Null* in 1978. The word *chaos* in this case is used as a "virtually meaningless" name free of the "anthropomorphic ideas of religion." Rather, it describes the thing responsible for the origin and continued action of events. Interestingly, the symbol commonly associated with chaos magick comes from the Elric novels by Michael Moorcock. Moorcock describes the symbol in his books as representing the chaos god that Elric of Melniboné and other characters worship.

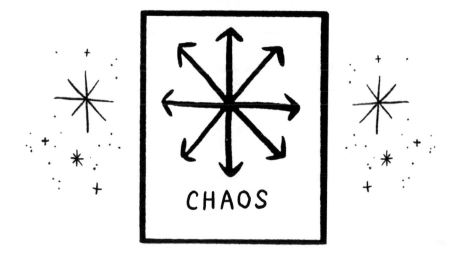

Following Carroll and Sherwin, there was Thee Temple ov Psychick Youth (TOPY), a magical group that formed in the 1980s. TOPY was like a creative commune, noted for its influence on youth culture in the '80s and '90s. One of the founding members, Genesis P-Orridge, was a member of the bands Psychic TV and Throbbing Gristle, and stated that TOPY was interested in "the meltdown of personal assumptions via guiltless sexuality and more formalized 'magickal' techniques derived from Austin Osman Spare, Brion Gysin, and Aleister Crowley, among others." TOPY wanted to achieve a magic designed for the "blank-eyed, TV-flattened, prematurely abyss-dwelling youth of the late 20th century," encouraging practitioners to create their own destinies, engender discipline, and pursue personal growth. TOPY created artwork as a form of magic and ritual, utilizing mediums like collage, cut-ups, sculpture, and music. TOPY uses the word *sigil* as almost a stand-in for *ritual* or *spell*. They write about performing sigils. TOPY leads us to ask questions around our assumptions of magic, especially sigils. How vast can a sigil be, and is there really a limit to what a sigil can be?

TOPY and Peter J. Carroll popularized the idea of the relationship between sex and sigils. They write about using masturbation or sex with a partner to charge sigils, and Austin Osman Spare lightly suggests that using personal pleasure can be a tool for charging sigils, but it's by no means the only method. Still, when most people or most magical practitioners (within and outside of chaos magick) talk about sigils, they suggest that sex (whether solo or with a partner) is an essential aspect to the sigil. Chaos magick and TOPY are largely why sigil crafting made its way into the mainstream, especially in terms of the methods we use most often to create them, and thus their methods for charging and activation are also in the forefront of popular understanding.

SIGILS AND IDENTITY

Sigils have been connected to identity, not just in being used as a name or signature. Sigils and symbols are used as personal markers and identifiers that represent part of our identity or sometimes our entire identity. Some symbols start off as a means to identify people without their consent but become sigilized through reclamation.

Gender Markers and Symbols

As a society, we have more or less agreed on what symbols are used to represent gender, at least in terms of a binary view of gender. One common representation is using the symbol for Mars to represent the male, and the symbol for Venus to represent the female. Even outside of a binary gender system, most symbols relating to gender utilize astronomical or astrological symbols. But what do the planets have to do with gender?

The precedent for using these symbols was set by Carl Linnaeus in 1751 when he used the symbols for Venus, Mars, and Mercury within the context of botany.

Traditional symbols for Mars/Male and Venus/Female

However, the roots of gendering the symbols of Mars and Venus and having Mercury as a nonbinary/androgynous symbol can be traced back to Ptolemy, who wrote about the masculine and feminine within the context of the planets in the second century CE. Ptolemy categorized the planets into masculine and feminine, making a note that Mercury is "common to both genders." Mercury would truly be shaped into an androgynous entity through the work of alchemists, who used Mercury as an aspect in their representation of the androgynous, which was considered divine. Alchemy and Hermeticism play a major part in how we view gender, especially within the magical and occult. It could be deduced that Linnaeus took inspiration from other books that carried forth the traditions of gendering different planets and bodies, and used these as further inspiration or copied them directly. For a long time, alchemy and science coexisted and were one and the same. Science and magic were just part of one another, so it wasn't uncommon to find individuals writing in a way that seems to marry the two. It seems that Carl Linnaeus was reading older texts, so while I won't say anything for certain, I think that there is a link.

The Kybalion (a significant Hermetic text, first published in 1903), states the Hermetic law of gender: "Gender is in everything; everything has its Masculine

Transgender symbol

and Feminine Principles; Gender manifests on all planes." The issue with a lot of these older occult texts that have undoubtedly influenced magical practices to this day is that they take a lot of words and phrases quite literally. Humans like patterns and repetition, so we perpetuate certain ideas throughout, including within magical schools of thought.

The transgender symbol that is most commonly used today was designed sometime in the 1990s. Holly Boswell drew it for Wendy Parker, who drew it for Nancy R. Nangeroni, suggesting that Nangeroni do something with it. Since its inception, the symbol has been used everywhere, becoming a powerful sigil that represents resilience, trans rights, trans identity, and more.

The problem with a lot of gender symbols is that they continue to refer to the gender binary and how different genders relate to male and female. Individually, every gender symbol is in itself a sigil, being a glyph that has taken on an innate meaning, being understood almost universally. As with any sigil, these symbols can be misused, misunderstood, politicized, radicalized, and stigmatized. As with any sigil, they are symbols that can take on individual meaning and potential.

You can use gender symbols in magic to affirm your gender, to help channel guidance regarding your gender identity (if you're questioning and need some support alongside more traditional methods), to love yourself, and to cast spells to protect trans people.

WITCHES' MARKS AND WITCH MARKS: PROTECTION AND SIGILS ON SKIN

Witches' marks and witch marks are not the same, and mustn't be confused with each other.

Witches' marks are protection symbols found throughout Europe, carved into the architecture of churches, houses, barns, and caves. Witches' marks refer to the apotropaic magic that exists, meant to protect the inhabitants, and to keep evil spirits (including witches) out of the home. These marks are found carved into stone or wood, usually near doorways and chimneys, or any space that might act as an opening to the outside world.

Witch marks (or devil's marks) are markings on a person that were used as a means of determining whether someone was a witch. Witch marks carry sigilic properties. These marks were believed to be permanent markings made by the devil. These marks were also believed to be magical or demonic teats that were used to feed the witch's familiar. If a person accused of witchcraft had a mark, it was seen as additional evidence that the accused individual was, in fact, a witch. The marks were pricked using pins, or witch prickers made specifically for the task, as these marks were supposed to be invulnerable and would not draw blood. Searching for witch marks was an excuse to strip, shame, and torture women.

These practices were most common in England and Scotland, but existed elsewhere in Europe during times of witch trials.

In modern times, we know that what would have been called a witch mark is usually just a mole or a birthmark. These marks can be removed through modern science (such as by freezing or plastic surgery) and can be an indicator of skin diseases or other ailments.

I have a mole on my buttock. I will sometimes observe it, considering what it would have been like to be accused of witchcraft, were I in the home of my ancestors during witch-trial times. I think about the horror of being stripped and searched, and that mark being violently pricked.

Any marks on our skin can become sigils. These marks, whether they are moles, birthmarks, scars, or tattoos, can be hidden and secret, or visible to the world. We can adopt these marks as symbols of strength, resilience, survival, or maybe even a source of personal power. Our bodies are a record of everything we've experienced, everything we've survived, everything we've loved, and everything we've consumed.

Part of me considers that I may need to get my mole removed, but I don't want to. I've grown to see it as my own witch mark, a source of energy and power, a part of my body that is objectively ugly or weird. My mole is magical. Sometimes I will anoint it, charging it as a source of witchy magnificence in a world where we're told that our bodies should be unblemished. Every scar on my body is a sigil, representing the power of the greasy meat suit in which I reside. These marks are witch marks and witches' marks. Both devil's marks and marks of protection and self. Maybe all those witch hunters did have it right. Maybe these marks are a source of power that others should be afraid of.

CATTLE BRANDS

The word *brand* stems from the Middle Ages Nordic word *brandr*, which means to burn down (as in to make a hot iron stamp on animals or objects). The word *branding* in terms of advertising and identity comes from the same place, and it has been suggested that totemism can be considered a precursor to branding (in the advertising sense). Totemism in the Neolithic era would emerge through the appearance of different communities having their own symbols devoted to animals, plants, or other things considered sacred.

While controversial (due to the discomfort and pain caused to the animal), there is no argument that cattle and livestock brands serve a particular purpose and take on sigilic or heraldic properties through their creation. The earliest evidence of marking cattle was found in Egypt, dating to around 2700 BCE. The purpose was the same as it is now: to indicate ownership so that the escaped or stolen cattle could be easily found. Brands are made up of simplified symbols, given names based on the letters and symbols used (like "bar over lazy T").

As I was researching this section, I was struck by how I never noticed the link between branding as in self-promotion or self-identification and branding as in marking cattle. I grew up on a sheep ranch, and then we moved to a cattle ranch, and we had a different brand in each place. I grew up going to cattle brandings, which are as much a social event as they are a practical use of community and teamwork. If you had cattle, you had a brand, and that symbol was as much a representation of your family as it was a practical symbol. Usually, at least one building in town would have cattle brands adorning the walls, representing families of the community, both present and past. My dad always had a belt buckle adorned with our brand. The symbol of the brand in rural communities took on a significant meaning beyond marking cattle to protect them from getting lost or stolen. The wall of brands in a town hall or seniors club took on an arcane appearance, manifested through marks created by pressing burning metal into the wood, the same burning metal that would mark the animals.

While I'm now vegan and I don't see myself ever attending a branding ever again, I'm kind of fascinated by the sudden realization that the word *brand* extends beyond cattle and my own worldview of what that word means. For most people these days, the word *brand* probably conjures up the idea of a logo or a label before anything else. They wouldn't be incorrect. The intention and the purpose of the cattle brand and the Nike logo are essentially the same, especially if you look at them through the lens of something like heraldry, where each house or family would have its own marking to denote that aspect of their identity.

MODERN SIGILS

Sigils are everywhere. As the world becomes more connected, symbols become more powerful and more charged. This takes them from just being a symbol, and into being a sigil. I call this sigilization, the accidental but organic transmutation of something visual into a magical symbol.

Grant Morrison wrote an incredible essay called "Pop Magic," which I believe is essential reading for any magical practitioner. It's a quick and easy read, and it breaks down a lot of information in a clear and understandable way. It talks about some types of sigils that are prominent in our modern world.

All logos are sigils, and they have a huge amount of psychic pull and effect on us. Corporate logos are as ubiquitous in our psyche as religious symbols or the alphabet. Morrison says, "Corporate sigils are super-breeders. They attack unbranded imaginative space. They invade Red Square, they infest the cranky streets of Tibet, they etch themselves into hairstyles. They breed across clothing, turning people into advertising hoardings. They are a very powerful development in the history of sigil magic, which dates back to the first bison drawn on the first cave wall."

This feels scary and intense, but Morrison (being the wise writer and magician they are) puts a clever spin on it: "Corporate entities are worth studying and can teach the observant magician much about what we really mean when we use the word 'magic.' They and other ghosts like them rule our world of the early 21st century. Track their movements over time, observe their feeding habits and methods of predation, monitor their repeated behaviors and note how they react to change and novelty. Learn how to imitate them, steal their successful strategies, and use them for your own. Build your own god and set it loose."

Corporate logos, and corporate ideas, can become sigils very quickly. They're easily recognizable symbols, something we all understand. Corporate logos and other viral sigils are almost more commonplace than religious symbols (those, too, being a type of sigil), and I'd hazard a guess that most children in North America understand the McDonald's Golden Arches before they have learned to read.

Hypersigils take the concept of sigils beyond simplistic symbols and static images and incorporate other aspects that flesh them out into something more real, more concrete. As Morrison writes, "The hypersigil is a sigil extended through the fourth dimension."

Morrison knowingly created a hypersigil through *The Invisibles* (which simultaneously consumed and recreated their life while it was being created), but a lot of other works of media are hypersigils. Alejandro Jodorowsky films and other high art/high concept films definitely feel like hypersigils. When you put that much intention into a film or any artwork, something is bound to happen. I would hazard a guess that if Spare had thought of the idea of a hypersigil, he definitely would have applied it to his own artwork.

Birth of a Nation (1915), Nazi propaganda films, and American war films are all hypersigils, shaped energetically into something more than just mere movies.

This type of media becomes a symbol, a direction, and an inspiration for people who see it. Similar to viral sigils of brands, propaganda films tap into a particular part of the psyche, altering mindsets and points of view. Sigils are meant to help direct energy and belief. Propaganda films take that idea and crank it up to eleven.

Propaganda films (and all forms of propaganda) are definitely sigils, but certainly in a negative way. After all, this type of media takes a specific intention and zeros in on the psyche to direct the viewer to believe something particular.

If viral sigils and hypersigils don't illustrate just how powerful sigils can be, I don't know what will. While all of this could be construed as pretty icky and uncomfortable, it's important to acknowledge, especially since it's kind of cool to think of the possibilities. If unsavory people can harness the power of sigilization for their purposes and create powerful sigils, what are we capable of? What can we do with our own sigils?

MEMES AS VIRAL SIGILS

Nowadays, a lot of propaganda is perpetuated through the medium of memes. Memes skirt the line between viral sigils and hypersigils, depending on what they are and how they are shared. This illustrates the complexity of sigils in our modern world, which is arguably a sign or symptom of how complex our world has become.

Meme was coined by Richard Dawkins in his 1976 book *The Selfish Gene*. The name itself has become autological (a word that describes itself), meaning that the word *meme* has become a meme unto itself. A meme can be likened to a gene in that it passes something on to another being, but instead of biological information passed through genetics, memes are ideas passed on through the senses. Memes transmit cultural ideas, symbols, and practices from one person to another. This occurs through a myriad of methods, from speech to writing to ritual.

Dawkins says, "If you contribute to the world's culture, if you have a good idea . . . it may live on, intact, long after your genes have dissolved in the common pool. Socrates may or may not have a gene or two alive in the world today, as G. C. Williams has remarked, but who cares? The meme-complexes of Socrates, Leonardo, Copernicus, and Marconi are still going strong."

We can argue that creating a meme in our world is achieving a type of immortality, and that memes are more important to our world than genes. Some theorists suggest that "memes should be considered living structures, not just metaphorically" because of their ability to self-replicate and mutate, as well as how they can respond to selective pressures (not unlike biological genes).

Internet memes are a more focused type of meme, in that they exist almost solely on the internet. That being said, those memes do expand outside of the digital space and into the physical or tangible. An internet meme is an idea, behavior, or style that is spread via the internet (this is why the word *meme* is more present in our collective lexicon). Internet memes are not only perpetuated by the average individual; they are also used for marketing as well as spreading political ideas or social activism. Even Russian trolls and bots have employed the phenomena of internet memes (and internet culture) to shift and shape views of individuals, manipulating their worldviews for gain. Thus, these memes end up accomplishing the same goal as a viral sigil. Memes can become sigilized through use.

The greatest example of this is Pepe the Frog. Pepe was created by artist Matt Furie in 2005. At this time, Pepe was one of several characters in Furie's comic *Boy's Club*. Pepe the Frog went from being an innocuous comic character to a symbol for white supremacy, all because of the internet. The documentary *Feels Good Man* illustrates the process of all of this in an intense and horrific way. The documentary even highlights how collective focus and directed thought can shape the world, suggesting that the use of Pepe as a hate symbol is part of what helped to make Donald Trump president. Of course, Trump's own sigils helped make that happen, including linguistic and visual identifiers such as the red MAGA hat. Soon, Pepe the Frog was transformed, stigmatized, and sigilized, and it was eventually added to the Anti-Defamation League's Hate Symbols Database.

SIGILS IN POP CULTURE

It's essential to discuss sigils within pop culture. Pop culture witches is one of my favorite topics, and pop culture is also one of the main methods in which most of us engage with or relate to witchcraft. While very few of us have taken the time to read a fifteenth-century grimoire, most of us have seen movies like *The Wizard of Oz* or *The Craft*. These depictions of witchcraft and witches are how we understand themes like magic, and they are often some of our earlier introductions to magic and the occult.

The popularity of witchcraft exists on a twenty-to-thirty-year cycle. There are some minor exceptions, but since the 1970s, witchcraft and witchcraft within popular culture has made a reappearance in media every two decades. The late 1960s and 1970s had the allure of sexy "black magic" witches adorning the covers of magazines in all their nude, skull-yielding glory, and started a rise in folk magic horror films (like *The Wicker Man* and *Blood on Satan's Claw*, among countless others). Magic was not only becoming more popular as an alternative spirituality, but it was permeating culture on a whole—which also led to a great deal of anti-witchcraft sentiment. Again, in the 1990s, a relationship between "girl power" and pop feminism created the perfect environment to introduce even more witches, with teen girls gravitating toward *Sabrina the Teenage Witch*, the coven in *The Craft*, and the magic of *Buffy the Vampire Slayer*.

Witchcraft never goes away, and it is always somewhat present in our culture (especially pop culture), but there seems to be something about certain generations that creates a craving for more magic and mysticism in our day-to-day lives, which always leads to the popularity of practicing witchcraft.

The occult has always been present in pop culture and popular media, from the witches in Shakespeare's *Macbeth* to the use of occult symbols in F. W. Murnau's 1922 silent classic, *Nosferatu*. The combination of magic and pop culture has a lot of interesting implications and possibilities. The concept of incorporating sigils, either real or manufactured, into films is also an interesting beast. On one hand, purposefully incorporating a sigil into something that is going to be consumed by a lot of people has the potential to charge the sigil more than any other method. The same goes for any hypersigils you might create. The more people interacting with or consuming a sigil, the more powerful it could (and typically does) become.

On the other hand, what of preexisting symbols that are regularly integrated into popular culture? Take, for example, the use of demonic sigils in horror movies. There's a possibility that using those symbols won't summon demons; but if that use of said symbols did summon demons, what would happen?

A certain level of risk comes with using preexisting symbols that are intended to summon a demon. Have artists or filmmakers who have incorporated demonic sigils into their work noticed strange activity in their lives? I'm not saying that tangoing with demons while shooting films is an absolute no-no or will lead to misfortune. But a lot of allegedly cursed films have involved satanic or demonic imagery and themes. Here's looking at you, *Rosemary's Baby* (1968), *The Exorcist* (1973), and *The Omen* (1976). Then again, one of the most cursed films is said to be *Anuk*, a would-be comedy that is believed to be so cursed it will likely never be successfully completed. Maybe satanic themes do not a cursed film make.

"But Lia," you might say, "you have plenty of demonic and maybe questionable sigils in this book. Are you worried about negative outcomes from that?"

A big part of me is always apprehensive about recreating certain sigils or markings, should summoning ancient evils be easier than I would have expected. I'm not even sure that I believe in demons in the traditional sense, but I opt to remain open to the existence of anything and everything, because I really don't know. So, to err on the side of caution, I do what any practical anxiety-ridden witch might do: I protect myself, and I set up precautions and fail-safes (including a number of secret sigils hidden in this very book).

I'm not writing this section to scare people away from incorporating anything esoteric or magical into their work. Rather, I think it's interesting to offer a crash course on sigils in film and pop culture to offer inspiration and information on the magical interacting with the mundane.

Film is going to be the means through which most people see sigils or magical markings, even briefly. Popular shows like *Supernatural* incorporate sigils into almost every episode, leading fans to use these symbols in their fan art, incorporate them into tattoos, and add them into all kinds of things that bring the sigil out of the silver screen and into our daily lives. There's something deeply mystical about that exchange. Generally, even if a sigil used in a TV show or movie or comic book isn't a historical symbol, it is based on preexisting ideas and symbols. So while it may not be a direct copy, there are some interesting implications in terms of the props department making a new sigil based on their own interpretations, which will then be taken to heart by the millions of people seeing it. I am of the belief that you can accidentally create a sigil, just as you can do anything by accident. If you can give someone the evil eye without meaning to, why wouldn't other forms of magic be possible, especially when you release what you have made into the world, into the hands and minds of millions of people who are going to feed it energy and attention? That is exactly how a sigil is made, after all.

The first appearance of sigils in film would likely be in the film *Nosferatu*, with a close second being *Haxan*. *Nosferatu* was produced by German occultist Albin Grau, who was also the production designer for the film. Albin Grau was a member of Fraternitas Saturni and imbued the film with mystical and occultic undertones. The most noticeable example is the mysterious and cryptic contract between the characters Knock and Orlak. Knock is shown reading the contract, which is filled with arcane symbols like magic squares, alchemical symbols, and symbols reminiscent of Angelic and Enochian letters, as well as sigils. Because of his understanding of the occult, Albin Grau likely made intentional decisions

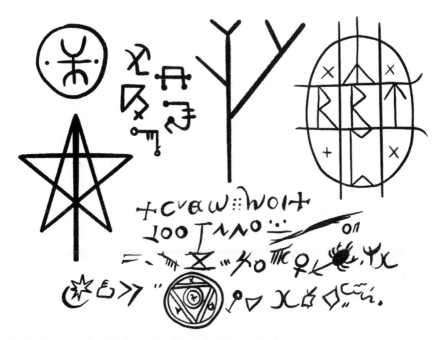

Sigils from *Lords of Salem, Gravity Falls, Horror Noire, Midsommar, Starry Eyes*, and *Nosferatu*

when creating the contract depicted in the film, especially given how long they show it on screen.

Haxan (The Witch) is a 1922 Swedish film which combines documentary with horror. The film offers an overview of the history of witchcraft in Europe, beginning in the Middle Ages. The film focuses predominantly on spells and witch activities, but the film does feature one occult marking: an apotropaic marking, which filmmaker Benjamin Christensen described as being inscribed on barn doors to prevent witches from entering. This marking is an octagram, or eight-pointed star. Similar symbols date back to Babylonian times, but the marking in question has persisted, continuing to be used as a Wiccan symbol to represent the Wheel of the Year.

Sigils regularly appear in more contemporary films, with both historical and made-for-the-film glyphs making appearances. In Ari Aster's films *Hereditary*

(2018) and *Midsommar* (2019), we see sigils being used as accents to the overall plot and themes of the story. *Hereditary* heavily features the Goetic sigil for the demon Paimon, a king of hell said to have knowledge over secret things and making spirits appear (among other powers, depending on the grimoire one is referring to). *Midsommar* features a number of runes and bind runes, as well as other occultic and mystical imagery that are not unlike sigils. The 2014 horror film *Starry Eyes* (written and directed by Kevin Kölsch and Dennis Widmyer) features a sigil made of a bisected pentagram, designed to represent the primary entity during the film (and also utilizes a number of real demonic sigils in the credits). Rob Zombie's *The Lords of Salem* (2012) prominently features a glyph designed for the film, meant to act as the film's visual representation of the witches and their devotion of Satan. *The Lords of Salem* is also noteworthy for including a musical piece that plays throughout, which I would consider to be an example of a musical or auditory sigil. This musical piece is made up of about eight notes, and it is played to control the women whose bloodlines can be traced back to the beginning of the town of Salem, including the protagonist of the film, Heidi LaRoc. The music is simple, but eerie, and casts a spell every time it is heard.

One of the most recent, and most prominent examples of sigils being utilized in a film is in the horror anthology *Horror Noire* (2021). In the second short, *Brand of Evil* (written by Ezra Claytan Daniels, and directed by Julien Christian Lutz), an up-and-coming artist, Nekani (played by Brandon Mychal Smith) is commissioned by a stranger to draw mysterious symbols, for which he is only given verbal instructions, and which he must complete by sunset. The job comes with the promise of a large sum of money, which Nekani takes, at the expense of completing a mural for the food bank he works with. The money pours in with each symbol he creates, but members of his community also start to mysteriously and brutally die. All of the symbols created for this short are new but inspired by preexisting symbols. The most noteworthy is the "midnight sun" symbol that Nekani creates and submits, despite others telling him that it's a neo-Nazi symbol. This fictionalized symbol is based off a very real neo-Nazi symbol, the Black Sun, which was adopted from ancient European symbols. Nekani ignores everyone's pleas to not do this job. Eventually, Nekani starts to realize the folly of his ways and pleads that he didn't know what he was doing. In response, his mysterious client says that "it's the corruption that gives the magic its powers," and that the symbols won't work unless the invoker knows the cost of his actions. While none of this is necessarily accurate when it comes to how sigils truly work, there is a level of truth to this story (not to mention the significant undertones of the narrative as a whole). *Brand of Evil* is most reminiscent of creating servitors through sigils, which isn't an inconsequential or insignificant thing to bring to the big screen.

Throughout the history of film (especially witch films), real witches have consulted on scripts and the work. Even before film, we have the legend of Shakespeare getting the spell for *Macbeth* from real witches, which led to the play being cursed. This kind of occurrence isn't uncommon. Even the film *Practical Magic* (1998) is said to be cursed, because the witch who consulted on the film was not happy about what she was offered in exchange for her consultation. Still, I would say it was worth it, as the scene where the sisters draw a pentagram with aerosol whipped cream is somehow one of the most authentic-feeling bits of magical ingenuity in any witch movie. *Simon, King of the Witches* (1971) is rumored to have had a real witch work on the film, but so little is now known about the production of this cult film. That being said, the film is very authentic in its approach to magic, down to the symbols and talismans that the protagonist Simon conjures. This film is actually the most interesting in terms of its use of the concept of sigils. Whereas most sigils are framed as two-dimensional glyphs or symbols, many practitioners pose the concept that anything that is a spell is a sigil. *Simon, King of the Witches* was written by someone who supported this school of thought, as we have a scene where Simon performs a ritual for a new friend of his, which includes a wooden plank or tray with four white candles, and a tin cup containing semen and human hair. Simon says an incantation to invoke certain gods, and says, "take this sigil into your depths."

Simon, King of the Witches is a detailed film that employs very real rituals and symbols to create an authentic film. The 2016 film *The Love Witch* (written and directed by Anna Biller) follows suit in terms of conjuring a world in which the magic comes from a very real and researched place. While Anna Biller may or may not be a witch, she did research every inch of the film's reference material, and even fabricated items like a pentacle rug and an altar (made to the specifications of Aleister Crowley) to invoke the right feel for the film. Even the spell book pages and pieces of paper that contain love spells written for victims of the tale contain very real symbols and concepts that would conjure real magic if used correctly.

I would be remiss if I were to write about film and sigils but not discuss queer American filmmaker Kenneth Anger's films. He created controversial shorts like *Fireworks* (a homoerotic work that led to Anger being arrested on obscenity charges) and occultic experimental films like *Inauguration of the Pleasure Dome* and *Lucifer Rising*. A member of the Ordo Templi Orientis (an occult order founded by Aleister Crowley), Anger was influenced by Crowley's descriptions of Lucifer and inspired by Crowley's poem "Hymn to Lucifer." *Lucifer Rising* depicts the arrival of the Aeon of Horus, believed to be a time of self-realization and self-actualization. Anger said, "Lucifer's message is that the key of joy is disobedience. Isis (Nature) wakes. Osiris (Death) answers. Lilith (Destroyer) climbs to the place of the sacrifice. The Magus activates the circle and Lucifer—Bringer of Light—breaks through." Throughout the film, Anger uses magical and sigilic imagery, including the unicursal hexagram (symbol of

Thelema), eight-pointed stars, images of Aleister Crowley, and flashing pictures that seem to capture momentary glimpses of spells. *Lucifer Rising* is believed by many to be a kind of spell or an invocation. The film has sigilic qualities, combining symbols, visuals, and a specific aesthetic to represent something grand and mystical.

Look for Sigils in Pop Culture

This section about sigils in pop culture was by no means exhaustive, and you'll likely start to see all kinds of magical symbols in movies, TV shows, and comic books. When you're consuming popular media, pay attention to the symbols and markings that appear. What about the symbol stands out? Does it feel significant? If you research the symbol, what kind of information emerges?

NINETY-NINE REASONS TO MAKE A SIGIL

1. To cast a spell
2. To help you see clearly
3. To be healthier
4. To save money
5. To trust
6. To be heard clearly
7. To be understood
8. To level up
9. To be better at something
10. To travel safely
11. For activism
12. For an important cause
13. For protection
14. For success
15. For abundance and prosperity
16. To help you improve at something
17. To make something magical
18. For inner beauty
19. For rest
20. For reflection
21. For fertility
22. For creativity
23. To make glyphs for tarot cards
24. To carry art with you in a nonliteral way
25. To enchant useful items
26. To pray
27. To call to gods
28. To bring in things you want
29. To hex someone
30. To keep negative spirits away
31. To keep unwanted, unneeded, or uninvited energy at bay
32. To make your day-to-day items magical
33. To do well at an activity
34. To motivate you
35. To inspire you
36. For protection in travel
37. To get a job
38. For manifestation
39. To banish someone unwanted
40. To keep cords cut
41. To invoke or evoke something or someone specific
42. To bind someone or something
43. For good luck
44. For healing
45. For strength
46. For vitality
47. For the benefit of others
48. For the benefit of the planet
49. To help inspire good
50. To protect yourself
51. To protect loved ones
52. To protect your animal(s)
53. To honor yourself

54. To conceal a secret
55. To keep something hidden
56. To get good deals on groceries
57. To save money on purchases whenever possible
58. To strengthen relationships
59. To strengthen your relationship with yourself
60. To cast a magic circle
61. For overall well-being
62. To get what you want
63. To heal wounds
64. To heal your heart
65. To remember to take your medication
66. To calm your nerves
67. To remember to breathe
68. To sell your things online
69. To be able to make money safely
70. To be able to donate money to important causes and mutual aid
71. To alleviate pain
72. To help you remember to exercise
73. To remember to take a break
74. To be okay with saying no
75. For bravery and courage
76. To call upon a particular deity

77. To communicate with spirits (deities, guides, angels, demons, ghosts, ancestors, Akashic masters, noncorporeal familiars, etc.)
78. To help you get answers
79. To pay bills without stressing
80. To pray
81. To transition
82. To come out
83. To live your truth
84. To figure out who you are
85. To help you confront someone
86. For justice
87. For balance
88. To help you find a familiar
89. To help you find a friend
90. To move away from something
91. To set boundaries
92. To enchant something precious
93. To make art
94. To practice your craft
95. To do something small for yourself
96. To be okay
97. To get what you need
98. To get what you want
99. To shape yourself into your ideal self

Chapter 4

HOW TO MAKE SIGILS

Thee are many reasons why someone might want to make a sigil. Personally, I have found that they're one of the most effective forms of magic.
They work incredibly well. I'm a natural skeptic, but I can't express the
number of times my mind has been blown by how functional a sigil can be. I
wouldn't blame you if you're reading this, thinking *Okay, sure* while rolling your
eyes. A lot of metaphysical stuff can take on an air of culty hyperbole, with an air of
"This will change your life!" That's truly not my intention here. I'm just being hon-
est. I'm writing a book about sigils because they have been my ride-or-die for a few
years now, and they have proven themselves time and time again. We've established
that sigils have been around for millennia; there must be something to them, right?

In more recent years, sigils have really hit their stride in terms of simplicity
and effectiveness. They've become easier to make and more approachable, and my
impression is that more and more people are using sigils because their magical
technology is functional and doable. Let me put it this way: tools don't typically
become popular because they don't work.

In this section, we'll be exploring a few different types of sigil crafting methods. I'll also describe how to charge your sigils, and how to use them in your day-
to-day life, both magically and creatively.

THE MAGIC SQUARE METHOD

Using magic squares to make sigils is the more traditional method for creating a symbol based on intention and goals. This method is more structured and mathematical, which is an excellent approach for anyone who is more analytical or has trouble (or a lack of interest in) making a graphic symbol. Creativity and the ability to conjure magical imagery can be a boon when it comes to sigil making, but it's by no means essential. However, as always, I encourage you to experiment and play if you're not making other types of sigils because it's difficult or challenging! Magic square sigils are a practical and logical means to make a sigil, and as long as you're well intentioned and put in the proper amount of work, there is the potential for satisfying results.

The magic squares (also called kameas) used in this method have been used for centuries. Each square is based on a planet. The planetary squares are Sun, Moon, Mercury, Venus, Mars, Jupiter, and Saturn. When I first learned all of this, I found it a *touch* confounding. Especially when I noticed that for most spellwork,

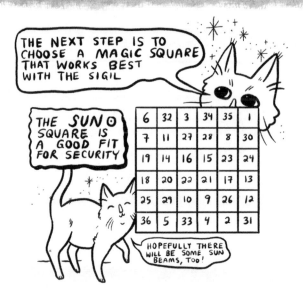

these are the only celestial bodies that are taken into consideration, usually under the pretense that the more distant planets don't matter (I'm sure plenty of astrologers would beg to differ). The reasoning for this is actually far more mundane: when magic squares were described in the sixteenth century, there were only eight known celestial bodies, including Earth. Written works on the subject at that time didn't really distinguish planets from other celestial bodies, thus the grouping of the sun and moon into the mix. So, it's not that the other planets don't matter. It's just that they hadn't been discovered by humans at this point in history. Like a lot of magical ideas, the magic squares have never been updated or expanded, which is probably for the best. While the math could be done to make squares for the other planets, those squares would be large, to say the least. Centuries of magicians and sorcerers probably opted for simplicity in lieu of completeness and accuracy. I will not be adding new planetary squares to the mix, because I am not that kind of person. I'm just here to tell you why things are the way they are, and how you can use them. But I commend anyone who decides to take up the gauntlet of making planetary squares for Uranus and Neptune. Maybe even Earth?

NEXT, CONVERT THE LETTERS INTO NUMBERS USING A CONVERSION CHART

THERE ARE TWO CHARTS YOU CAN USE. JUST MAKE SURE ALL THE NUMBERS FIT IN YOUR CHOSEN PLANETARY SQUARE!

SECURITY ≈ 15339927

NOW IT'S TIME FOR THE FUN PART!

START WITH THE FIRST NUMBER. IN THIS CASE — NUMBER 1!

6	32	3	34	35	1
7	11	27	28	8	30
19	14	16	15	23	24
18	20	22	21	17	13
25	29	10	9	26	12
36	5	33	4	2	31

DRAW A CONNECTING LINE FROM NUMBER TO NUMBER, CREATING ONE LONG LINE.

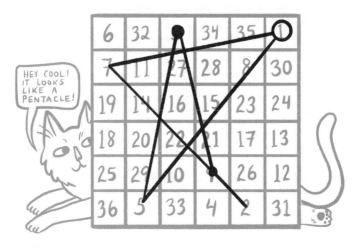

CLOSE THE SIGIL BY RETURNING
TO THE FIRST NUMBER. TA-DA!
THE SIGIL IS COMPLETE!

Making Magic Squares

You will need:

- A pen
- A printout of magic squares
- Access to conversion charts
- Tracing paper

Optional

- A calculator
- Extra paper

....

Note: You can also make magic squares using a drawing app on a phone or tablet. Take a photo of the magic squares in this book or scan them in, and then use multiple layers in the drawing app to draw over the magic square. I usually do this myself, because I'm never organized enough to have all of my tools in one place, but I *do* have all of the necessary pieces on my iPad.

....

This method is good for those who are more analytical and detail oriented, and those who like to have a step-by-step process. If you're slightly panicked at the idea of being creative, this is a good method. The idea of getting creative and making art (especially intuitively) can be really intimidating, especially since we can get hung up on the question of whether we're doing it "right." By contrast, this method of sigil making removes a lot of that fear, providing a clear order of action.

The first thing you'll want to do is decide what you want to make a sigil for. In this method, it can be better to choose a word or a short phrase, because the longer the phrase, the more lines you will need to form the sigil. A shorter phrase will make this process easier, because unlike other sigils, you won't really edit the finished glyph. Once you close the sigil, that's the symbol. The result will be something geometric in appearance, with intersecting lines.

As with any sigil, you can also use it to create a glyph meant to represent someone specific. To do that, you would use a name (your own or someone else's). If you wanted to put more intention into your sigil but don't want to end up with too many lines, you could prepare your phrase the way you would when using the Austin Osman Spare technique: remove all of the vowels and repeating consonants to distill your intention down to fewer letters. You could also use the mantra/incantation method (see page 102) to create a shorter phrase. There is always potential to mix and match techniques to get the most bang for your buck out of your sigils.

For the sake of explanation and simplicity, I'll use a single word to demonstrate this technique. From there, you can perfect your own technique and experiment further.

Once you've figured out your word, decide on a planetary square that will best suit the sigil you're making. Each planet carries different energy and rules over a different part of our life. For example, if you're making a sigil for luck, you may want to choose the Jupiter square, as Jupiter rules over expansion and concepts like luck. If you're making a sigil for intuition and divination, you may choose the Moon square. Different factors can go into deciding which square is best, but ultimately it all depends on your intention and what you think would make the sigil the strongest it can be.

Next, convert the letters from your word into numbers. There are a few ways to do this, depending on the size of square you'll be using. I like to use a conversion chart that goes up to 900, because it gives a bit more wiggle room. However, if you're using a smaller chart (like Jupiter, for instance) you might just opt to use a 1–9 chart. You can also use numerology and assign each letter of the alphabet a number, from 1 to 26. If you need a smaller number, you add the digits together (for example, $Z = 26$, so $2 + 6 = 8$). The goal is to be able to fit a number representing each letter inside the square you have chosen. You can do whatever you need to make that happen (this part is pretty loose, honestly).

Once you've converted all of your letters to numbers, on the magic square you've chosen to work with, find the number that represents the first letter of your word. Lay the tracing paper on top and mark the spot. The first number is often denoted by drawing an open circle.

Then find the next number and draw a line that connects that number to the first. Repeat this process with each number until you've drawn a line to each number that is part of your word. At this point, draw a line from your last number to your first, connecting them and completing the sigil.

What if you have multiples of the same number in a row? This is ultimately up to you. Some sigil crafters will use different markings, like semicircles or curved lines, to denote that the number is being used multiple times. Personally, I don't make any special markings, except for the first number, which I denote with a filled-in circle. Sometimes I end up removing that circle, depending on what I need the sigil for.

CONVERSION CHARTS

1	2	3	4	5	6	7	8	9
A	B	C	D	E	F	G	H	I
J	K	L	M	N	O	P	Q	R
S	T	U	V	W	X	Y	Z	

1	2	3	4	5	6	7	8	9
A	B	C	D	E	F	G	H	I
10	20	30	40	50	60	70	80	90
J	K	L	M	N	O	P	Q	R
100	200	300	400	500	600	700	800	900
S	T	U	V	W	X	Y	Z	&

THE SEVEN
MAGIC SQUARES

4	9	2
3	5	7
8	1	6

SATURN

4	14	15	1
9	7	6	12
5	11	10	8
16	2	3	13

JUPITER

11	24	7	20	3
4	12	25	8	16
17	5	13	21	9
10	18	1	14	22
23	6	19	2	15

MARS

6	32	3	34	35	1
7	11	27	28	8	30
19	14	16	15	23	24
18	20	22	21	17	13
25	29	10	9	26	12
36	5	33	4	2	31

SUN

VENUS

22	47	16	41	10	35	4
5	23	48	17	42	11	29
30	6	24	49	18	36	12
13	31	7	25	43	19	37
38	14	32	1	26	44	20
21	39	8	33	2	27	45
46	15	40	9	34	3	28

MERCURY

8	58	59	5	4	62	63	1
49	15	14	52	53	11	10	56
41	23	22	44	45	19	18	48
32	34	35	29	28	38	39	25
40	26	27	37	36	30	31	33
17	47	46	20	21	43	42	24
9	55	54	12	13	51	50	16
64	2	3	61	60	6	7	57

MOON

37	78	29	70	21	62	13	54	5
6	38	79	30	71	22	63	14	46
47	7	39	80	31	72	23	55	15
16	48	8	40	81	32	64	24	56
57	17	49	9	41	73	33	65	25
26	58	18	50	1	42	74	34	66
67	27	59	10	51	2	43	75	35
36	68	19	60	11	52	3	44	76
77	28	69	20	61	12	53	4	45

THE AUSTIN OSMAN SPARE METHOD

There's a very clear reason as to why this is *the* method that most people use to create their sigils. It's easy and straightforward, and there aren't any restrictions beyond needing something to write with—but even then, if you're a visual person who can conjure strong psychic pictures, you might be able to create sigils using visualization alone.

The goal, in the simplest terms, is to take a phrase and distill it into a visual symbol. Spare created this method because it allows anyone to achieve the goals that he lays out in his *Book of Pleasure*, even if they're unable to achieve vacuity (a total clarity and emptiness of the mind). Through the creation of the sigil, the desire of the sigil maker passes the ego and the conscious mind and goes straight to the subconscious, allowing the desire to become a reality. In this method, there's a great deal of flexibility and creative liberty. That's a big part of why it's become so popular: the method is flexible and lacks the rigidity of older forms of sigil crafting. The Spare method of sigil crafting is kind of like making a crazy quilt as opposed to a more traditional quilt with a repeating pattern. One has more room for spontaneity and creativity, and the other requires a bit more order and attention, but at the end of the day, both are functional works of art.

Start by creating a phrase for your desire: a goal or a wish, something you want to manifest or bring into reality.

I encourage you to try this method even if you're intimidated by the idea of creating. Sometimes it's hard. You might get stuck, because it's easy to get worried about whether or not you're doing it right. That is fair, but eventually you will learn to trust yourself and know that the symbol you're making is powerful. It can be scary at first, but trust in the mystery and give it a try. If it doesn't work, then banish it and try again. You're doing this for you, and there's no judgment. You're not being tested. You won't be graded on your sigil making.

To start, write a phrase that describes what you want. It's best to write an affirmative statement, a phrase that presents your ideas as if they've already happened and are already a reality (see the "Affirmative Statements and Magic Making" section on page 124).

Once you've made the most banging phrase you could possibly imagine, go through it and remove all of the vowels: A, E, I, O, and U. Whether or not you include the "sometimes Y" as a vowel is up to you. I usually decide whether I'm going to include the Y based on the intention of the sigil. More often than not it gets removed, but if a word starts with a Y, I might be more inclined to include it.

After all the vowels are removed, go back and remove any repeating consonants. Once you're finished, you're left with a seemingly random string of individual, nonrepeating letters. Now for the fun part: turning those letters into a sigil.

You have two options at this point. One option is to go letter by letter, combining them into some kind of glyph, ensuring that every letter is represented. The other option is to go letter by letter, breaking each letter down into its root lines. So, for example, a letter R would become one vertical line, one diagonal line, and one open semicircle. Once you've broken down all of the letters, you would then combine those into a symbol.

I tend to go with the first option. Sometimes I won't even go letter by letter. I've made many a sigil by intuitively shaping it, just knowing that the entire phrase is represented in that symbol. The more proficient you are at sigil making, the more flexible you can be. Sometimes you'll want to be diligent and detail oriented, but other times you may churn out a quick sigil to accomplish a fairly basic goal representing something relatively inconsequential.

Once you've created a glyph, you can go over it, edit or reshape it, or redraw it into something until it looks truly magical and powerful and gives you that ooh-la-la sensation.

THE AUSTIN OSMAN SPARE (AOS) METHOD IS FUN + CREATIVE!

START WITH A PHRASE YOU WANT TO MAKE INTO A SIGIL

LET'S MAKE A PROTECTION SIGIL—

MY SPACE IS PROTECTED & SECURE. MY BOUNDARIES ARE RESPECTED.

MY SPACE IS PROTECTED & SECURE MY BOUNDARIES ARE RESPECTED.

REMOVE ALL OF THE VOWELS

AND THEN ALL OF THE REPEATING CONSONANTS

YOU'LL BE LEFT WITH A FEW LETTERS

FOR EXAMPLE MSPCR TDBN

CIRCULAR KEYS

The below are examples of different kinds of circular keys.

Golden Dawn Rose Cross Key of Sigils

The Hermetic Order of the Golden Dawn was founded in 1887 and was dedicated to the study of the occult, metaphysics, and paranormal activities. A great deal of modern witchcraft and occultism can be traced through the Order of the Golden Dawn, which in turn based its rituals and teachings on Hermeticism, Kabbalah, and other ancient magical methods.

One of the primary symbols used to represent the Golden Dawn is the symbol of the Rose Cross, which has origins with the Rosicrucians. Members of the Golden Dawn used the Rose Cross to develop a means to create sigils. The so-called Key of Sigils and Rituals represents the forces of the twenty-two letters in Nature, divided into sections of three, seven, and twelve petals. The inner three petals represent the elements of Air, Fire, and Water (this combination also represents the element of Earth, because they have a relationship to Earth in that they are part of it). The next seven petals represent the seven planets, and the next twelve represent the signs of the zodiac. Each petal is denoted by a Hebrew letter that corresponds to the ring of petals. The practitioner would make their sigil based on Hebrew, starting with the first letter of the word, and connecting each letter with a line, in the same method used when creating sigils with magic squares.

Attempts have been made to use the Rose Cross circle with Roman letters, but there isn't a one-to-one exchange between Hebrew and Roman letters, and there are only twenty-two spaces. When I tried creating sigils using a circle that someone incorporated Roman letters and phonetic sounds into, I felt like a certain level of intentionality and magic was lost. If you are going to use the Golden

Left: Golden Dawn's Rose Cross
Right: Roman alphabet version of Rose Cross key

Dawn's key, I recommend familiarizing yourself with the Hebrew letters and working with it as it was originally intended.

Other practitioners and occult groups (including Thelema) have created methods that employ the same idea, using circles to create sigils, including a three-ringed key that looks similar to the Golden Dawn's Rose Cross but arranged differently to accommodate the twenty-six letters of the Latin alphabet. These structures work, but they don't really click with me, because the construction doesn't feel overly intentional, especially when compared to the Golden Dawn's Rose Cross. S. L. MacGregor Mathers's writing on the Key of Sigils describes a complex, carefully arranged structure. By comparison, the anglophile/Roman alphabet version is rather unsatisfying. Thus, I created a circle key of my own for your use.

CRUCIFIXVI Circular Key

In the vein of the Golden Dawn, I used numerology and careful consideration to decide how many letters would go in each ring and how I would arrange the twenty-six letters.

The center ring is made up of five spots, with one spot for each of the magical elements (Earth, Air, Fire, Water, and Aether/Spirit). The middle ring is made up of nine spots, representing each of the nine planets (Mercury, Venus, Earth, Mars, Jupiter, Saturn, Uranus, Neptune, and Pluto). The outer ring has twelve spots,

representing the twelve signs of the Zodiac (aligning with the Golden Dawn key). The letters are arranged based on Chaldean numerology to provide a higher vibration to all of the letters.

To use this key to create sigils, use the same general method as with magic squares. Create a short phrase or select a single word, and draw a connecting line from letter to letter.

Perfect Circle Key

Another method consists of arranging all of the letters in a perfect circle, and then drawing a line from one letter to another (not unlike certain types of spirit boards).

ADDITIONAL NOTES ON SIGIL MAKING

When you start practicing any method of sigil making, you may want to approach it with a to-the-letter sensibility. This means following instructions exactly as they are written until you feel you are practiced enough to start executing sigils with more fluidity and personal style. When you are learning anything, it's not a bad idea to follow the instructions step-by-step. Think of following a recipe: the first time you make it, you want to follow the recipe exactly. However, the more you make it, the more comfortable you become. You understand the techniques and start to intuitively know that the recipe doesn't have enough salt or spice for your taste. You start to make modifications and alterations based on personal experience and personal taste.

Approach magic with this kind of attitude. Follow instructions and really understand the ins and outs before you start to experiment freely.

When I make sigils, I go back and forth between following the instructions exactly and working intuitively—it depends on what I feel the sigil calls for. After all, the way you create a sigil could have a direct impact on your spellwork. Sometimes I will ensure with absolute conviction that every letter is represented. Other times, I will distill it and then immediately start making a magical symbol. Both kinds of sigils are equally effective, but sometimes more attention to detail is necessary—think about the difference like how you approach baking a soufflé or macarons as opposed to making chocolate chip cookies. The former requires an exacting approach, each step is finicky, and failure is an overwhelming possibility. The latter is more forgiving and accommodates individual preference more easily.

You'll know when you feel comfortable enough to start experimenting and adopting variations to sigil making. You're not ready until you are, like anything in life. Of course, you may be inclined to follow a certain pattern forever because that's your nature. Any way that you incorporate sigils into your magical practice, and how you continue to create them, is valid, and it will work.

OTHER FORMS OF SIGIL CRAFTING

Here are other options for making sigils that we haven't yet covered.

Mantra/Incantation Method

This is a way to create a sigil that can be spoken, sung, or written as a word. Think of it as a way to create a magical incantation. You can also use this method to create a short phrase that you can use in the crafting of a magic-square sigil.

Write out the phrase that you wish to turn into a mantra or incantation. Remove all of the repeating letters (both consonants and vowels).

Allow words and sounds to form. Rearrange the letters until a magical phrase reveals itself. Charge it as you desire, and use this verbal sigil the way you would any other sigil (including being written down).

Pictorial Method

Draw a symbol drawing of what you wish to happen. For example, In *Liber Null &*
Psychonaut, Peter J. Carroll uses a depiction of an adversary being restrained to
create a sigil for that purpose. The resulting drawing looks like a poppet being
bound with nails. You can use any image that represents your desire or wish.

Once the drawing is created, take the individual shapes and lines and begin
to distill the image until you have a more simplified glyph.

I like using this method to transmute preexisting art or imagery into a sigil,
using art that represents what you want or represents a correspondence that you
wish to incorporate into your spellwork. For instance, say you want to make a
spell dedicated to Venus. You could take a famous artwork, like Botticelli's *The*
Birth of Venus, and convert it into shapes until you have created a sigil dedicated
to Venus.

You could also use the pictorial method to sigilize a favorite tarot card as a
way to embody its full meaning, which could then be used in spellwork or a special ritual.

Process of creating a sigil for a safe home using the pictorial method

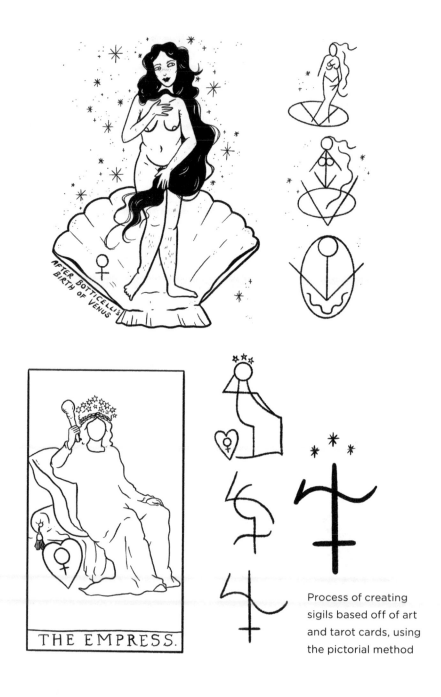

AFTER BOTTICELLI'S
BIRTH OF VENUS

THE EMPRESS.

Process of creating
sigils based off of art
and tarot cards, using
the pictorial method

CHANNELING AS A TOOL IN SIGIL CRAFTING AND CONJURING MAGICAL IMAGERY

Channeling can take a lot of practice, but it can be worthwhile. Channeling is the practice of letting a spirit communicate with or through you. Most channeling is performed by mediums (including yours truly), but everyone is capable of channeling spirits. Every human has psychic abilities. Think of psychic abilities like drawing. For example's sake, I'm going to make a generalization. Pretty much everyone on the planet has the capability to draw a picture, even if it's through unconventional means, like a disabled individual holding a pen in their mouth or with their toes. Some people don't consider themselves to be good at drawing, but if you convince them to play a game like Pictionary, or you ask them to draw something specific, pretty much everyone on the planet will be able to conjure some type of image (with the exception of people with debilitating illnesses that make such things virtually impossible). The point is, we're all more or less capable of holding a drawing utensil and making a combination of lines that come together to form a recognizable picture. Psychic abilities are kind of the same. While it may not be easy or pretty for most people, and there are factors that render it extremely difficult for some, every human has the potential to tap into psychic gifts, should they choose to do so.

Like art making, psychic abilities come with practice. It's exceedingly rare for someone to wake up and be a Michelangelo, but we can all start with drawing basic shapes, eventually working up to creating elaborately rendered works of art. Just as you can practice and study drawing every day to improve, you can do the same with developing your psychic abilities. As with art, you'll also develop your own unique style of psychic channeling.

Earlier, we discussed ancestral knowledge and how you can tap into that wealth of information. One of the ways you can access ancestral knowledge is through channeling. When you channel, you call spirits, and those spirits give you information to help you.

I like to use the all-encompassing term *spirits* to represent all of those non-corporeal beings who come through when we channel: gods, angels, demons, familiars, ancestors, departed loved ones, guides, Akashic masters, and teachers. A wealth of information can come through channeling, and sometimes it's a mixed bag of who or what will have information for you. Each of us has a unique team of spirits who are our spiritual and magical cheerleaders and teachers, and they're always excited to talk and touch base. Sometimes they even hold important symbols, and I've even received sigils to pass on to the person I'm reading or channeling for.

It can be difficult to connect with your spirits at first, especially if you don't normally communicate with them. Fortunately, there's a wealth of information out there, and you don't have to go full-on medium to connect with your own spirits. It can just take some warming up to open up the channels so that you can hear them and receive messages. The way you receive messages will also vary. I receive my messages predominantly through clairvoyance (clear seeing, which I experience by seeing clear messages in my mind's eye), clairaudience (clear hearing, which I experience by hearing from outside of myself), and clairsentience (clear knowing, which comes from just inherently knowing something or being given information, like a download), but there are many different ways to receive messages from spirits.

You can start by talking to your spirits on a regular basis. You can leave offerings, make an altar to call them, and practice raising your vibration. You might ask your spirits for signs or symbols that you should watch out for. You could ask them to communicate with you through dreams. If you feel stuck, there are a wealth of guided meditations that help you connect with spirits. Generally, they'll likely be focused on connecting with your spirit guides, but you can still use the methods to connect with your whole spiritual crew. Eventually, you'll be able to start connecting with your spirits through channeling, and you'll be able to ask them to give you sigils or symbols that will be of use to you.

Even if you choose not to connect with spirits, you can still use psychic abilities to form sigils. To strengthen your psychic mind for this, start by sitting comfortably in a quiet place. You might choose to use binaural beats or white noise to dull any outside distractions if you have trouble focusing. Once you're ready, form mental images of shapes. Visualize the shapes. Form a triangle. Form a perfect circle. Form a square. Visualize these shapes as clearly as you possibly can. Hold the shapes in your mind. Eventually, you might choose to form more complex images, like a detailed picture. Exercise your ability to form images and hold those pictures in your mind. Then play around with the possibilities of those shapes. What if you practiced making Austin Osman Spare–style sigils, but only using your mind's eye? What if you concentrated on a purpose or intention and on the absolute blackness behind your eyes until an image or symbol spontaneously appeared? What happens if you draw these symbols on paper, and meditate with them? What happens if you take the images you have conjured through intuition, and refine them further? What will your experiments yield?

Channeling Your Spirits

Sit comfortably in a quiet room. If you have trouble quieting your mind like I do, you can put on background music like binaural beats or chanting. I'll usually find a binaural beats track that is at least an hour long, or go to the app Insight Timer and set it to unlimited, selecting one of the background tracks that includes humming or chanting. The object isn't to go into a trance; it's to quiet your mind and ground yourself so that you can open yourself up to information from beyond. I will usually call to the spirits around me, inviting them to speak or send images. What pictures appear in your mind? Record what you see, smell, and hear. Be aware of your senses, and use your intuition to determine where the messages are coming from. Sometimes you will experience only your own thoughts and memories, but the more you engage with this kind of channeling, the more you will be able to distinguish when messages are coming from other beings, even in your day-to-day life, when you're not actively channeling. Start by doing this for five to fifteen minutes.

After you are done, thank the spirits, drink some water, and go for a walk or do something else that helps you ground back into your human body (I'll often make myself a snack and watch something funny). Channeling can be really exhausting, so as with anything magical or metaphysical, it's important to take care of yourself after.

USING RANDOMNESS AND DIVINATION
AS TOOLS TO CREATE SIGILS

In occultism and witchcraft, different methods of divination read the outcome of chaos and randomness of actions, to receive messages from the Aether and beyond. The following is a list of a few methods of divination, taken from a list made by John Gaule in 1652.

Aeromancy, by the air

Alphitomancy, by meal, flour, or bran

Arithmancy, by numbers

Astragalomancy, by dice

Botanomancy, by herbs

Capnomancy, by smoke

Carromancy, by melting of wax

Cleromancy, by lots

Dactylomancy, by rings

Demonomancy, by the suggestion of evil demons or devils

Geomancy, by earth

Gyromancy, by rounds or circles

Hydromancy, by water

Lecanomancy, by a basin of water

Lithomancy, by stones

Macharomancy, by knives or swords

Oniromancy, by dreams

Onomatomancy, by names

Onychomancy, by the nails

Ornithomancy, by birds

Psychomancy, by human souls, affection, will, or religious or moral disposition

Pyromancy, by fire

Roadomancy, by stars

Sciomancy, by shadows

Spatalamancy, by skin, bones, or excrement

Theriomancy, by beasts

There are countless forms of divination, and this partial list from Gaule doesn't even begin to exhaust the methods. One common thread between a lot of these types of divination is randomness. Most forms of divination involve reading the results of an action that triggers a random response. For example, casting lots or runes. We act as a conduit to allow something random to happen. We have set a certain number of controlled variables, such as the stones chosen, how or where we throw the stones, and so on. But ultimately, the result is random. We then use these results to read or divine information based on a question or an intention.

We can divine the answers, but we can also use these tools for other practices, including making sigils. Instead of asking a question, we can set an intention for the symbol we wish to create. This idea came to me while I was on a drive with my husband. I was tired, and I closed my eyes and entered that liminal space between waking and sleeping. During this time, the idea of using runes or lots to create sigils came to mind. I've since practiced this method, and I found the result to be incredibly magical. The symbol created (inspired by a tarot reading) felt really potent. Once I had this sigil, I charged it as I would any other sigil created by more traditional methods.

Casting Lots, Casting Sigils

- A small collection of items to throw. *You might choose runes, crystals, coins, bones, or anything you have on hand. The items you choose don't need to be inherently magical, because they will become magical through this process. I would recommend having between six and twelve items, but you can use your intuition to decide what is suitable. For the sake of simplicity, I'll be writing about this in the context of runes, because it'll be clearer to discuss it from a singular example.*

- A safe place to throw your runes. *You may choose to have a casting cloth or a small rug or placemat. You don't want to break or lose any of the items you're throwing.*

- A notebook or pieces of paper

- A writing utensil of your choice

1. Select your divination tool. I used pewter Witches' Runes, which work the same way as traditional runes (they just have different imagery).

2. Set an intention for your sigil. You might want a sigil to help you get a new job, to help you focus, or to protect your home. Whatever the intention, say it to your runes. You might speak it aloud, or whisper it. You could place your runes next to your heart while holding the intention in your mind while you take a few deep breaths.

3. Once your intention is clear, throw your runes!

4. After all of the runes have fallen, remove any that are upside down or blank. If you are not using runes, this might not be relevant. You can choose not to remove any of the items. Use your intuition. You'll know which, if any, are not relevant to the sigil you are creating.

5. On a piece of paper, plot a map showing the locations of the remaining runes. This will look kind of like a constellation. I use a marker to roughly draw dots to represent each rune.

6. Connect the dots! You can connect them in the order you drew the dots, or choose intuitively. Maybe you will see shapes that click with you and feel really good for the sigil you'd like to create. Make sure you connect the last dot to the first dot, so that the entire shape is closed.

7. Play around! Similar to the Austin Osman Spare method of making a sigil, this method allows you to redraw and reshape the lines you've created in order to craft a symbol that feels truly magical.

8. Charge your sigil. Using the methods described later in the book, charge and activate your sigil so that it can start doing its work.

This method feels really true to me. Maybe it's because I conjured it, but there's something about it that just works. One of my regular incantations is "Trust the mystery." I'm not good with change or the unknown, which I think a lot of people can relate to. But magic is all about unknowns! "Trust the mystery" transmutes my fears into a workable sense of curiosity. Curiosity is such a virtue for us magical practitioners; when we open ourselves up to new possibilities and ask questions, we open ourselves up to stronger magic and the ability to harness magic in unexpected ways. Creating sigils by casting lots or using any form of divination that thrives in the random and chaotic allows us to use the unknown. This opens us up to the Aether, to the Universe, to Spirit, to God. Whatever you want to call it, it's a powerful energy that exists all around us. Why not try to pull in some of that intensity? Why not make the unknown our home?

Creating sigils through methods that harness the random is to put ourselves in liminal spaces, finding ourselves in the betwixt and between. As a nonbinary person, it feels right to use this kind of energy. Through the random and the liminal, what we set intentions to create could go either way. This results in sigils that are completely out of our control. That feels cathartic, especially in terms of making sigils to aid in areas we can't control. There's some kind of sympathetic magic about using something we can't control in order to control what we can't control. It feels like potent magic.

The first sigil I crafted using this method was created through the intention of making a symbol to help me unblock. As I mentioned earlier, this was inspired by a tarot reading in which it was made abundantly clear that there were energetic blocks and I was standing in my own way. What better way to unblock and get out of your own way than to step aside and let other energies decide what should happen? Sometimes the best way to get back on track is to completely let go.

Using these chaotic, random methods to create sigils works because they remove a lot of factors that prevent us from letting magic happen. The key is that we need to forget what a sigil means. Sometimes if we create a sigil that starts with words, we cling to the language that we used to bring it to life, and that halts the sigil from integrating with our subconscious. A sigil is like a wild animal. Sometimes we're inclined to try everything in our power to tame it, to *make* it come to us. We find ourselves focusing on our desires and what we want, rather than realizing that it's this forcefulness that's preventing things from moving forward.

This random divination method of creating a sigil is like leaving out food for an animal that has already come to us. The animal is still uncertain, but the work that we need to do to befriend it is different. Whereas other types of sigil making are about conjuring a sigil and then forgetting about its meaning, this random creation doesn't have anything to forget. We just need to foster it.

Other methods of sigils work incredibly well, so I don't want to misconstrue anything. I make sigils, post about sigils, and write about sigils because they work. There's room to experiment and approach older forms of creation (whether magical or mundane) with curiosity. We are always allowed to approach older methods with questions and see if we can figure out a new way to do it. Sometimes the old way isn't better or even necessarily logical. Often, the reason for doing anything boils down to "it's the way it's always been done," which is never a good reason to do something. If you can intuit or intentionally develop a new and interesting way to do spellwork or create art or do anything, why not? Magic is incredibly old, but that doesn't mean that we can't continue to shape and evolve it.

Conjuring Sigils Through Random Patterns

Set an intention for a sigil, and observe different places and ways you might divine a sigil. Here are some other ideas for creating sigils using randomness:

- Record the movements or shapes of birds, and create sigils based on their patterns.
- Look for shapes in a scrying glass.
- Draw shapes with your eyes closed.
- Use the elements (Air, Earth, Fire, and Water) to make patterns on paper.

What types of divination can you use to create sigils? What are some different ways you can create sigils? How can you spark your own curiosity, in order to make room to experiment and try something different? How can you use spontaneity to create magic?

AUTOMATIC DRAWING

Automatic drawing (or writing) is the practice of falling into a trance or meditative, gnostic state and letting your subconscious or spirits guide your hand. This can be used as a method of channeling, through which you can create sigils or other magical drawings. Automatic drawing can be a means of incorporating magic and the spiritual realm into your artwork or writing. Austin Osman Spare, Rosaleen Norton, and other occult artists have used automatic drawing throughout their careers.

INCORPORATING OTHER SYMBOLS IN YOUR SIGILS

I mentioned earlier that you can incorporate pre-existing symbols into your sigils as you craft them. This is easiest to do with the Spare method of sigil making, and has the possibility of making sigils more focused. However, I do think that sigils are more successful when you focus your energy into the meaning of the sigil itself and develop a connection with it.

Sometimes adding additional symbols (such as astrological symbols, pentagrams, crosses, whatever) can help boost the magic of the sigil, but you also don't want to get hung up on aesthetics or making it "pretty." We want to make a sigil *magical*, a term that isn't synonymous with aesthetically appealing (despite the world trying to condition us to think that it is). After all, sometimes focusing on the aesthetic of something and making it beautiful rather than just letting it *be* feeds into patriarchal and capitalist ideas that something has value only if it's visually appealing. Women, femme, and feminine folk are force-fed this idea the most, and there's zero reason why we should perpetuate such ideas in our witchcraft or magical workings.

I want to make it very clear that *there is nothing wrong with adding symbols or wanting to make your sigils pretty.* You do you, and you do sigils your way! The most important part of any magical working is doing it *your* way, and making it work your way. But I recommend perfecting a technique that works for you and observing how sigils work for you *before* you get hung up on always making pretty sigils. This applies to all magical workings in general.

It's important to remember that magic doesn't need to be pretty or acceptable or gentle. I'm a firm believer in letting my magic be dirty and gritty and vulgar and obscene and whatever else it needs to be in order to be functional and give me results. My most successful spells have always been those that have been passionate but well planned and practical. This is something that we don't see on social media (sometimes we don't see it on the internet at all) because it's not pretty or appealing. Crying while invoking a goddess, cleaning grave dirt from under your fingernails, or mixing black salt with your bare hands isn't exactly cute. Plus, usually when we practice this type of magic, we know that sharing any details risks breaking the spell or dissolving the magic.

As with any practice, magical or otherwise, let your sigils come from a deep place of self. Don't be afraid to be gritty and punk rock in bringing your sigils to life. Art is messy, and you can't spell *witchcraft* without *art*.

CULTURAL APPROPRIATION

I have been asked on a number of occasions how to avoid cultural appropriation when making sigils. It's an important consideration because we don't need more cultural theft, appropriation, or misappropriation.

Here's the thing: it's really hard to appropriate something else if you're creating your own sigils. You'll naturally fall into your own style, and it may be visually similar to other types of sigils and magical symbols. This random coincidence that might occur is not cultural appropriation.

You can incorporate preexisting symbols into your sigils, but if you're not sure if you can use something, just err on the side of caution and don't use it! If you don't think you have ownership of something, then you probably don't. But, as in art creation of any kind, if you're creating something entirely new and not drawing inspiration from anything, you don't really need to worry about cultural appropriation. It's your creation, and it's your magic.

Ultimately, symbols made up of simple lines and shapes are going to look like other things. Sigils are ultimately primitive in design. Primitive mark making is something we share as humans, just as we all have some type of language, whether it's written, verbal, or nonverbal. It will always have something in common with another language, and that's just because we're all human beings with a need for the same thing.

Bottom line: don't get hung up on the idea of cultural appropriation when it comes to sigil making. If you create art and you're not worried about cultural appropriation, then you shouldn't be worried when it comes to your magical mark making when crafting sigils.

SECRECY AND SILENCE

One of the benefits of practicing sigil magic is its overt practicality and the fact that you can keep it secret. For centuries, witchcraft was condemned and punishable by death. In many parts of the world, the fear of witchcraft is still prevalent. Over the last two decades, thousands of people in countries around the world have been imprisoned and killed, primarily in developing countries, all because of the suspicion of witchcraft.

Cultural and individual fears of witchcraft come from a history of misogyny, homophobia, transphobia, classism, and racism. Most people who are accused of witchcraft are women, with a few exceptions throughout history.

Being able to practice witchcraft or magic safely is a privilege. As with any spirituality or religion, the ability to practice openly means that you are in a safe place, with little or no judgment. We live in a world that is constantly unstable, and most spiritualities have been persecuted at some time or another (some more than others). You don't need to be spiritual in order to practice witchcraft. You do not need to treat it like a religion.

But there is a primal fear in humans that makes us afraid of the unknown. We are always afraid of what we don't understand, and many of us do our best to understand or educate ourselves, but the reality is, we all have moments when we have strong reactions to the unfamiliar. You can be as woke as possible, but you are still going to have moments where you react to the other.

The witch has always been the other, someone who is different, who doesn't align with the status quo or what is generally accepted as okay. As witches and as magical practitioners, our history is intertwined with the fear of people who don't understand us or those who are like us.

It is because of this history that we need to acknowledge that it is amazing that we are able to read and write spell books, wear pentacles and crystals, and share our views and spells online. It's unprecedented. How powerful is that? Every now and then, our world goes through its cycles and we find ourselves in a period where spirituality and the occult are more mainstream. We're in one of those periods now. The cycle aligns with culture and the celestial bodies and seems to cause an awakening in a lot of people. Suddenly, magic is real, and spirituality is important. We start to see and understand things differently. Then more of us are collecting crystals, burning herbs, and working with the moon. It's incredible.

It's magical that we are able to lean into the unknown and the other, and embrace the metaphysical parts of our lives. We just need to remember that it is a privilege, and we are fortunate.

Even in places like North America and Europe, a lot of witches and magical folk are in positions where they may not feel comfortable or safe openly practicing witchcraft. And they shouldn't have to feel that they need to practice in full view of others. Not everyone has to be open about their craft, just as no one is required to share their entire life. Social media has kind of shaped us into a "pics or it didn't happen" society, even with parts of our lives that are more deeply personal. There are a million reasons why someone won't want to be open about their practice, and every single reason is valid.

In witchcraft, there is the idea of the Witches' Pyramid, also known as the Four Pillars of the Witches' Temple. Originally referred to as the Four Words of the Magus or the Four Powers of the Sphinx, the concept is credited to Éliphas Lévi, who wrote about the idea in his 1896 book *Transcendental Magic*. The four pillars are "to know," "to dare," "to will," and "to keep silence." Later, Aleister Crowley would expand upon this to add "to go." Eventually, all of this was distilled down and integrated into witchcraft and Wicca. The applications of the Witches' Pyramid can be pretty broad, including being used as a component and structure for spellwork. In that, we can apply the pyramid to how we craft sigils and how we practice magic as a whole. It's a valuable concept to consider.

> **To know** is to have knowledge and an understanding of magic and of all aspects of the craft. The more the practitioner knows, the more they understand and the more successful and powerful their magic will be. Know yourself, know your power, and know your abilities.
>
> **Key words: Information, awareness, and understanding**

To will is to be certain and have conviction, to know that your magic is real and believe wholeheartedly in the magic you create. It is the ability to conjure and use power and energy, and be able to maintain focus and intention.

Key words: Focus, direction, and confidence

To dare is to let go of fear and doubt, to experiment, play, try, and experience. It is a willingness to push past barriers or meet a challenge, and to transmute your fear into confidence and magic.

Key words: Courage, bravery, and moving forward

To keep silent is to hold the wisdom that not everything needs to be shared, and sometimes it is better to allow deep understanding of your magic and craft. There is power in keeping secrets. There is power in understanding our magic and ourselves, in a deep and silent way, unknown to others.

Key words: Listening, protection, and secrecy

SECOND NATURE VERSUS EASE

Sigils work and are effective, and that's why people use them in their magic. However, this doesn't mean that they're easy. Magic shouldn't always be easy. Sigils work, but that doesn't mean that every sigil will be successful. Do the work. Don't get stuck in *how* you work. Don't give up on something because it proves to be difficult. If we only ever do something because it's easy or convenient, we'll render ourselves unfulfilled. Yes, you could eat instant ramen every day because it's cheap and quick and easy. Or you could accept that you're not being nourished if you do that, and learn how to do more. Learn how to do other things that seem difficult, and let the previously difficult become second nature. Make mistakes, and learn from those mistakes. Keep a notebook to record your successes and failures.

Magic is the act of changing the world around you by shifting energy and selecting desired outcomes. Magic has the potential to be earth-shattering and world-moving. You might transform your entire being. None of that should come from something easy.

Challenge yourself. Sigils are profound because they are simple and seemingly easy, but there is still a lot of work to be done when you begin trying to understand them. You can challenge yourself and level up indefinitely. You can challenge yourself to master different methods of sigil crafting. You can challenge yourself to try completely new things, going bigger and grander, transmuting your sigils into massive spells, rituals, comic books, or movies. Once you've mastered the basic techniques of something, you can only move up. Once something feels easy, expand and continue to challenge yourself and your magic. If you are able to walk, there was once a time when you only crawled, but you eventually stood. You were scared to let go and learn to walk and move on your own. Let your instincts take over. Let go of the familiar and the safe. Let go and let your magic be more, be bigger, be wilder.

Are sigils challenging you? Good! It's a good thing to challenge ourselves. Question yourself and why you do something or why you don't. Challenge yourself and experiment so that you—and your magic—can expand and grow.

Curiosity and belief are essential to magical work. They are essential to being a good magician or witch or whatever you call yourself. Shift yourself out of the mundane world. Don't think *Oh wow, what a coincidence!* when something unreal happens. Think instead *It worked! I knew it would.* Think *Magic is real!* Think and know without a doubt. There are no coincidences. There is only magic.

Skepticism has become a dangerous concept, more like devout fundamental nonbelief and knowing that something isn't real than like mere questioning. People who call themselves skeptics are often absolutely certain that something isn't real or isn't possible. Don't close yourself off to the possibilities of the unknown and the magical. Just because you haven't seen or experienced something doesn't mean it isn't real.

Take a moment to reject all banal mundanity, and shake loose the shackles of realism and so-called logic. Say yes to not knowing. Say yes to altering reality. Say yes to cryptids, aliens, and fairies. Say yes to the possibility of possibility. Say yes to magic being real.

AFFIRMATIVE STATEMENTS AND MAGIC MAKING

Something about the Universe/Aether/Spirit/God (whatever you see as a higher power) tends to listen pretty intently to strong verbal statements. This is why you should think twice before you say something like "I never win" or "I have the worst luck" or "I'll never find true love." The Universe does listen. Instead, learn to say things in an affirmative, clear, specific way.

When making a phrase to create magic for, I think of episodes of the *Twilight Zone* series from the sixties. A couple of episodes involve wish making. Every single time, because it's the *Twilight Zone* and it's all about comeuppances, the wishes fail because the individual making the wish wasn't specific enough. In the episode "The Man in the Bottle," Arthur Castle, an antiques dealer, comes across what appears to be a wine bottle, but it turns out to be a genie, who offers Castle and his wife four wishes. First, they ask the genie to fix a broken glass cabinet to prove the genie's power. Next, they wish for a million dollars in cash, but after giving money away and being presented with a hefty tax bill, they are left with $5. Finally, the genie warns of the consequences and suggests that they should think very carefully before making their next wish. Castle wishes to be in a position of power, where he can't be voted out of office, in a modern and powerful country. Lo and behold, Castle is turned into Adolf Hitler and transported to the last days of World War II. He wishes to be returned to his old life. All in all, Castle and his wife are left with nothing except for a repaired cabinet, which Castle ends up breaking by accident. The lesson is to be careful what you wish for, an ideology can be applied to any part of magic, but it's especially prudent when it comes to the language we choose to use in our magic making, including sigil making. The takeaway? Apply careful consideration when deciding what to make a sigil for. Consider the possible consequences. Consider if it's something you really want, or if it could be misinterpreted on a cosmic level. My husband once asked for $4,000 for something specific, and it happened—but it came in the form of an offer to increase his credit limit by that exact amount. It worked, but it's not exactly what he meant. Language is a tool we use to turn ideas into truths that permeate our world. Language is a magical tool in itself, and we need to remember that the intention behind our words can have a major impact on the outcome.

For example, making sigils for "I have a job that pays me well and treats me fairly" is going to be more effective than "I want a job." It's more clear, plus it's more specific to what you actually want. The more specific you are, the more effective your magic will be.

It is important to note: *if bad things are happening, it's not because you manifested them.* In the spiritual world, there is a lot of toxic positivity, which starts to heavily imply (or flat-out say) that people who are not doing as well in life are in that position because they manifested it, or weren't thinking positively, or weren't speaking in affirmational ways. Sometimes people are in circumstances where they can think as positively as humanly possible, but they are in a position that is built to keep them down. Toxic positivity is built on a structure of privilege and entitlement. Sometimes things suck. Sometimes there isn't a way out through spirituality or magic, because the cis-hetero capitalist white patriarchy has purposefully built things to keep certain people down.

It's easy to say "be positive" if you're white, straight, and cis.

I am not here to tell you that being affirmative or positive will make everything go right. I'm not here to say that you can magic your way out of shitty situations. But I am here to say that you have the autonomy and the power to try, and positive statements do work. Even our brains respond to affirmative statements. Magic is older than the patriarchy, and that magic is potent.

Affirmative statements work because the more clear you are to the Universe/God/whoever, the more clear you are to yourself and to your intentions and desires. It's not even about being positive, per se. It's about being direct and being clear. It's punk rock as fuck to tell the world that you deserve something. You have the power to demand that your needs be met. You have the right to say what you want. You have the right to use your voice like the powerful tool it is.

Chapter 5

MAGICAL ALPHABETS

There is a plethora of magical alphabets and writing systems that can be used in your magic as a whole or incorporated into sigils. You can use any alphabet or writing system on the planet (including fantasy alphabets, or those of your own creation) and those offered here do not scratch the surface of writing systems in the world. I'm choosing to focus on those that have been or continue to be used within the context of magic.

RUNES AND BINE RUNES

Runes are letters in runic alphabets, which were used to write various Germanic languages. The Scandinavian variant is known as futhark, and the Anglo-Saxon variant is futhorc, both having variations and changes in some letters and sounds.

The earliest runic inscriptions are from about 150 CE. During the Christianization of Central and Northern Europe (roughly 700 and 1100 CE, respectively) the use of runic alphabets was replaced by the Latin alphabet, but in some areas the use of runes persisted (especially in Northern Europe). The three main runic alphabets are Elder Futhark (approx. 150–800 CE), Anglo-Saxon Futhorc

(400–1100 CE), and the Younger Futhark (800–1100 CE). From there the alphabets break down further depending on region and use.

Runes can be worth understanding and knowing, especially if your ancestral roots are in Western or Northern Europe. Runes have a place within the context of magical discussion and theory not only as an alphabet but also as divination tools, in which stones or pieces of wood (or any small object) are marked with the different runes. It is worth noting that runes being used as a divinatory tool is a relatively new magical invention, and isn't as old as a lot of people are led to believe. This doesn't invalidate runes as a divinatory system by any means, but working with runes as a form of lot casting isn't an ancient art. The first instance of someone writing about runes in this manner was Ralph Blum in 1982, which led to the popularity of runes being used as a divinatory tool. There are allusions to divination in earlier texts that could be interpreted as casting runes, but there is no solid evidence.

Bind runes are a ligature of two or more runes, combined to form a single conjoined glyph. Historically, these were typically used to represent the name of someone, but sometimes they're cryptic. Most bind runes are seen on runestones, large carved stones around Europe. Nowadays a lot of pagans and witches do use bind runes as part of their magical practice and to create sigils.

There is an unfortunate side to runes, however: Nazis and white supremacists have ruined the party. Some runes and bind runes make some people uncomfortable because of the use of runes and runic writing by white supremacists. A few runes are listed on the Anti-Defamation League's Hate Symbols Database, including the Jera rune, the Life rune, the Othala rune, and the Tyr rune. Regarding the Jera rune, they say, "It is one of a number of runic symbols that white supremacists have appropriated but is also commonly used by non-racist modern Norse pagans, so care needs to be taken in its evaluation."

Context is everything when it comes to these symbols, and it's important to remember that white supremacists *do not* own these symbols, and you are not prevented from using runes or bind runes in your sigil work. Pagan spirituality does not owe white supremacists these symbols, and we shouldn't give up runes to white supremacists and neo-Nazis. Racists don't get to take ownership over something that is significant within spirituality. Racists don't get to have whatever they want.

Examples of bind runes

THEBAN

Also known as the Honorian alphabet, or the witches' alphabet, Theban was first published in Johannes Trithemius's *Polygraphia* (1518) and attributed to Honorius of Thebes, but its origins are ultimately unknown. It is used in modern witchcraft and Wicca, acting as a substitution cipher to hide magical writings in one's Book of Shadows or a grimoire.

EGYPTIAN HIEROGLYPHS

True Egyptian hieroglyphs do not function as a one-to-one substitution cipher, though many scholars and writers have created what could be described as a pseudo-alphabet that fulfills this need. In his *Complete Book of Witchcraft*, Raymond Buckland offers one such hieroglyphic alphabet, but it's not really true to the written language of the hieroglyphs. Still, one could use ancient hieroglyphs within their magical workings and sigils, whether they be symbols for letters, sounds, or a logogram (which represents the object that it resembles; i.e., a pictorial representation of a specific thing).

PASSING THE RIVER

Passing the River is a Hebraic Kabbalistic writing system based on the ancient Hebrew alphabet. Agrippa describes this alphabet in *The Third Book of Occult Philosophy* (1553). It consists of twenty-two letters and is similar to the Celestial and Malachim alphabets.

ANGELIC/CELESTIAL

This is not to be confused with the Enochian alphabet. The Celestial alphabet was also recorded in Agrippa's book, along with Malachim. The script and language are said to have been invented in order to communicate with angels. There are twenty-two letters, most of which are based on Hebrew names. It is occasionally used in rituals.

MALACHIM

Malachim translates from Hebrew to *angels* or *messengers*. Malachim is derived from the Hebrew and Greek alphabets, and it still used by some Freemasons.

OGHAM

Ogham (also spelled *ogam*) is an early medieval alphabet that appeared in Ireland at least 1,600 years ago. It was used to inscribe Primitive Irish onto stone monuments and is the oldest form of the Gaelic languages. Similar to bind runes that appear on carvings around Europe, the vast majority of ogham inscriptions represent names of individuals. Ogham is sometimes referred to as the Celtic tree alphabet, because of the high medieval Briatharogam, which corresponds the individual letters to various trees. The alphabet originally consisted of four families of characters, characterized based on the style of stroke, with a series of supplementary letters to make up additional sounds.

PICTISH

Pictish is an extinct language spoken by the Picts, who existed in eastern and northern Scotland from late antiquity until about 1100. It may be related to ogham. Two variations of Pictish are used in modern witchcraft. One variation of Pictish is the swirl script, inspired by the Pictish stones found in parts of Scotland. The other is PectiWita, which refers to a Scottish Solitary tradition. PectiWita was passed on by Aidan Breac, who taught the tradition until his death in 1989. Raymond Buckland recorded some of his teachings, including information on Pictish runes and "swirls."

ENOCHIAN

Enochian was channeled and produced by John Dee and Edward Kelley between 1581 and 1585. Dee described this alphabet and language as "angelic," but never formally named it. Since John Dee recorded the alphabet, other writers and magicians have added additional flourishes to the letters. For the sake of posterity, the version I have included below is copied from John Dee's notes.

Chapter 6

CHARGING YOUR SIGIL

To charge your sigil means to activate it. The goal is to fuel it up with energy and power so that it can go out and do its work. This is also your opportunity to embody the deep, nonverbal, and metaphysical meaning of the symbol you have created (remember, you want to forget the literal meaning that you created the sigil around).

It's become pretty widely accepted that the best way to charge a sigil is to masturbate or have sex and think about the sigil at the point of orgasm. There are a few reasons why this isn't true, and we can probably let this idea die. The idea of an individual *having to* orgasm in order to charge their sigil can be a bit alienating to some. We're all different, and a lot of us have trauma, or the inability to orgasm, or a disinterest toward orgasm. There are so many reasons why someone might not want to orgasm, and why someone might not be interested in adding a sexual element to their magical practice. No one should feel incapable of utilizing a magical tool. Magic, like anything else, can be made accessible to anyone and everyone who feels called to it. Like any tool that exists in the world, it can be modified to fit most needs or levels of ability. There should never be caveats in magic (or any spiritual path) that make practitioners feel unwelcome or unable to do something.

Charging a sigil just means applying a certain level of focus, allowing you to activate it but also giving the opportunity for the image to pass by your ego and go into your subconscious. This can be done in many ways. Meditation is a good option, and there's nothing wrong with orgasm, but it's really up to the individual.

One common method is to burn the sigil. This is a great idea, because you're literally applying a lot of physical energy to the sigil. My only personal question around this method is, what do you do with the ashes? In my own magic, I usually only burn something to release or to hex (burning is a great method for banishing people or ideas), so when I'm done I might flush the ashes or dispose of them in a place far away from my home. But maybe you're doing a spell for protection, and it feels good to burn the sigil. It'd be counterintuitive to throw those ashes away or flush them. What's something intentional that you can do with those ashes? You could incorporate them into a protection salt, allowing you to work the sigil into a physical manifestation of the goal you're trying to accomplish through your sigil. You could bury the ashes in the pot of a protective plant. You could make the ashes into an ink to use in your magic. There are a lot of options, but my suggestion is to make the decision as intentionally as you made the sigil. Still, when in doubt or uncertain, casting any spell residue into the winds or discarding it at a crossroads is a good option.

You can charge the sigil by doing something physical that helps you activate the sigil. Grant Morrison suggests something like bungee jumping or another activity that helps you feel a lot of adrenaline. Orgasm would be another physical option, if that is something you want to do. You can go for a walk or a run, or do yoga. I've charged a sigil while getting a tattoo, by focusing on the image of the sigil every time I felt like the pain of the tattoo was too much. That being said, I do not encourage utilizing pain, especially since this might suggest ideas of self-harm. Still, if you know that you're going to go into something painful, like getting a tattoo, a piercing, or a deep-tissue massage, or even childbirth, you could work with this pain. I do not encourage making yourself feel pain with the intention of charging a sigil. Do not incorporate self-harm into your practice, especially when charging your sigils. You know what your own story is, and you can make your own choices. While I will never condemn anyone who self-harms, I do not encourage self-harm of any kind.

At this point, my personal go-to for charging sigils is to focus on the symbol and breathe with it and meditate with it. This charges the sigil with a certain type of energy that is directional and wholly focused on the sigil itself. What works best for you will likely vary. Like anything magical, you will find a method that aligns with you and your purposes.

NINETY-NINE WAYS TO CHARGE OR ACTIVATE A SIGIL

1. Carve it into a log that you are going to burn.
2. Write it on a piece of paper and burn it.
3. Flush it down the toilet.
4. Masturbate.
5. Bungee jump.
6. Get a tattoo.
7. Draw it in the air while dancing to a favorite song.
8. Use a wand to "draw" it on the walls in your home.
9. Meditate.
10. Go for a walk.
11. Have a picnic with friends.
12. Breathe in the hot steam of a coffee.
13. Go for a swim.
14. Make a meal.
15. Do a tarot reading.
16. Make art based on it.
17. Hike in nature.
18. Take some deep breaths outside.
19. Smoke.
20. Play with your animals.
21. Clean your house.
22. Exercise.
23. Do yoga.
24. Paint the sigil.
25. Draw the sigil.
26. Make a collage with the sigil.
27. Sit with a candle.
28. Howl, yell, or scream.
29. Sleep with it under your pillow.
30. Visualize it coming true.
31. Visualize the sigil becoming powerful.
32. Dance.
33. Get your heart rate up.
34. Slow your heart rate down.
35. Sit with a supportive crystal.
36. Tell your plants about it.
37. Embroider the sigil.
38. Bake a special food.
39. Draw the sigil in the air using a stick of incense.
40. Call on spirits to charge it.
41. Go on a roller coaster.

42. Go to a concert.

43. Tell your animals about it.

44. Write out the Fibonacci sequence, following the shape of the sigil you created.

45. Have a shower.

46. Do an activity that inspires the purpose of the sigil.

47. Break something.

48. Bury it.

49. Cry.

50. Laugh.

51. Have sex.

52. Have a nap.

53. Go for a run.

54. Draw the sigil on your altar.

55. Draw it on the sidewalk.

56. Make a playlist.

57. Watch or listen to something scary.

58. Mindfully drink a glass of water.

59. Sing along to a favorite song.

60. Light a match and think about the sigil as it burns.

61. Draw the sigil and rip it up in a fury.

62. Plant something.

63. Sing.

64. Focus on it.

65. Forget about it.

66. Do something different.

67. Draw the sigil with water-soluble ink, and run the paper under water until the ink bleeds and washes away.

68. Draw the sigil in the sand.

69. Draw the sigil in dirt.

70. Draw the sigil on various skipping stones, and skip them into a river.

71. Envision the sigil bringing your goal to fruition.

72. Collaborate.

73. Imagine.

74. Draw the sigil in your spit.

75. Draw the sigil in your menstrual blood.

76. Get angry.

77. Create an incantation, and repeat the words over the sigil.

78. Draw the sigil in snow.

79. Think about the sigil every day before you go to sleep.

80. Think about the sigil every day when you wake up.

81. Have a ritual bath.

82. Shave your legs or face.

83. Draw down the moon.

84. Talk to the moon, the sun, and the stars.

85. Draw the sigil over and over again.

86. Hold your hands over the sigil and infuse it with energy.

87. Place the sigil under a significant moon phase, and let the moon charge it.

88. Look at the sigil through a mirror.

89. Carve the sigil into something significant.

90. Engage with the sigil in a meaningful way.

91. Defecate or urinate.

92. Burn the sigil with special herbs and incenses that aid the purpose of the sigil.

93. Apply a face mask or do other self-care rituals.

94. Carve the sigil into ice and let it melt.

95. Freeze the sigil.

96. Watch fireworks.

97. Do something repetitive but mindful, like knitting or crochet.

98. Draw the sigil into the back of your animal with your fingers.

99. Ask your familiar to help make the sigil a truth.

Witches' Black Salt

Witches' black salt can be very useful in charging your sigil.

You will need

- Salt (any type)
- Ash from burning a protection sigil (or any positive sigil that you want to continue to work with)
- Other ashes, such as incense ash or ash from burning herbs; or charcoal or other powders that won't rot or spoil

Mix the salt with the ashes. You can do this by stirring carefully with a spoon or wand, or you can put the contents in a closed jar and give it all a good shake. You can always add new ashes to your blend, or top up the salt. Your black salt can be an ever-evolving blend that you're always adding to. You can even burn incense sticks directly into the salt by standing them up in your jar, and then picking out the leftover bamboo when the incense is burned down.

BANISHING SIGILS

In magic, if you don't believe in something or don't want something to exist in your world anymore, you can practice techniques that remove this unwanted entity from your life. Techniques relating to this do not include focusing on the thing, making it impossible to escape your mind. This goes for symbols and sigils that we don't want present in our life. If you don't want to contribute to the sigilization of something, exorcise it from your life and encourage others to do the same.

This idea goes along with an idea present in a lot of chaos-based sigil crafting: banishing or destroying the sigil once it has served its purpose.

A lot of chaos magick texts (including Peter J. Carroll's *Liber Null & Psychonaut*, and Bluefluke's *The Complete Psychonaut Field Manual*) talk about using sigil making to create or conjure magical beings, entities, or servitors. In the case of a servitor, you manifest an entity to help you complete a task or goal, but once it has completed its task, you must delete or banish it. You may also do this with other sigils you may have made, especially if the sigil isn't working the way it should, or the sigil has run its course. But generally, banishing or destroying a sigil isn't essential, and most sigil making doesn't call for it. However, maybe you want to banish a sigil that you haven't created.

Earlier, we discussed viral sigils: corporate logos or memes or stigmatized symbols that are inherently toxic to our psyches and well-being. Sometimes we don't want these in our life, but we as humans have a really bad habit (especially in the current age of the internet) of sharing what we don't like. Instead of ignoring what we don't agree with or removing it from our life, a lot of us have the tendency to share it all over the internet, blasting it because of how bad it is. The result? More people are aware of it. The image or the idea is more present in the individual and collective psyche. More people embody the idea. Remember when Trump became president in 2016? There were theories that the only reason Trump won the presidency was because he was so present in the mind of the average voter. Even if you share something as a joke or because it enrages you, the idea is still reaching more people. That idea becomes charged and sigilized. Suddenly, that *thing* is more a part of our world than it would have been if we'd ignored it and not given it attention. Even parodying the image or symbol results in further charging. Those designs that permeated our minds during the reign of Trump, like "Make America Goth Again" or "Make America Smart Again" and a hundred others, existed to poke fun at the absurdity of the original MAGA hat, yet the result is almost the same as if people had just worn the actual Trump insignia. The intent isn't the same, but it contributes to the energy fed into that symbol and what it means.

None of this is to say that ignoring something will make it go away. That's generally not true. If you're being attacked by a bear, ignoring the bear won't stop it dead in its tracks. However, in the realm of sigils and the magical, the way to remove what you don't want to see (whether it's a symbol, or otherwise) is to ignore it and to remove it from your brain. You can even make a sigil to help with this.

Whether it's a sigil that you've created or a sigil that you no longer want to see, the banishment is the same. It can be a complex ritual, or you can simply stop acknowledging its existence. In magical thinking, you must focus on making the idea you don't like absent from your brain. Let the image fade from your mind. Cease to speak the name. Cease to recognize the symbol for anything other than what it is; let the symbol become a series of random, meaningless markings.

YOU KNOW HOW TO MAKE SIGILS—NOW WHAT? SO WHAT?

You have crafted your sigil. You intend to make many, many more. But what now? How do you apply your sigils to your everyday life, and how do you continue to utilize them in meaningful ways? As with any magic, how you apply or use your sigils is really up to you, and it likely depends on why you chose to use that sigil. Sometimes your interaction with your sigil is a one-and-done kind of thing, and you won't put much thought into it. Other times, you want to incorporate that sigil in meaningful, continuous ways. It's all valid, and that's part of what makes sigils so very, very cool.

NINETY-NINE PLACES TO PUT A SIGIL

1. Drawn on a mirror with magic water (moon water, sun water, or water infused with crystals)

2. Carved into a candle for spellwork

3. Drawn on the back of a wristwatch

4. Tucked inside a phone case

5. Drawn on the bottom of shoes

6. Embroidered into cloth

7. Drawn onto water bottle with magic water

8. Drawn onto skin with essential oil or perfume

9. Drawn onto skin with moisturizer, makeup, or other product that will blend into your skin

10. Drawn onto the bottom of your cup with a bit of tea or coffee before filling it up

11. Stirred into your coffee or tea with a spoon

12. Drawn on a wall before painting

13. Carved into beams or doorways (if you own the building. I am not here to recommend vandalism.)

14. Left on community bulletin boards or in free library

15. Carved or drawn on a pet's ID tags

16. Drawn on the back of the identification tag a suitcase

17. Drawn on the underneath of a doormat

18. Drawn on dryer sheets or wool dryer balls, using essential oils or moon water

19. Drawn on windows with magic water

20. Incorporated into artwork

21. Drawn on mix CDs or tapes

22. Drawn on plant pots

23. Crocheted or knitted designs

24. Iced on a cake

25. Carved into baked goods

26. Formed with your hands during meditation or exercise

27. Tattooed or drawn with henna or temporary ink on skin

28. Printed or drawn on clothes

29. Carved onto a cauldron

30. Engraved onto metal tools or jewelry

31. Carved or burned into wooden kitchen tools

32. Drawn on bandages or casts

33. Drawn on bay leaves

34. Used as a signature

35. Printed on a custom-made phone or iPad case

36. Incorporated into woodworking

37. Incorporated into ceramics

38. Incorporated into nail art

39. Incorporated into wire art

40. Sculpted or incorporated into other three-dimensional artwork

41. Drawn in the sand on the beach

42. Reproduced with stones or crystals (especially in a garden)

43. Written on money

44. Carved into petroglyphs

45. Carved into geoglyphs

46. Drawn on rolling papers (make sure whatever you use to draw it is safe to smoke)

47. Carried around in a wallet

48. Set as the lock screen or wall-paper on devices

49. Drawn on the back of picture frames

50. Drawn on crystals

51. Made into stickers

52. Made into bookmarks

53. Drawn on lip balm or lipstick tubes

54. Drawn on tarot deck box

55. Quilted

56. Used as battle vest insignia

57. Made into jewelry

58. Woven

59. Recreated in how you tie your shoelaces. Tie your shoe laces to look like the sigil you created

60. Used in shibari

61. Drawn in snow

62. Drawn in soil

63. Shaped with pressed flowers and leaves

64. Carved or scratched into medication

65. Drawn on a medication bottle

66. Drawn under a rug

67. Drawn on trash, recycling, and compost bins

68. Drawn on pet food bags or treat bags

69. Drawn on Post-it notes

70. Drawn at the beginning of journals

71. Incorporated into magic circles

72. Drawn in salt during rituals

73. Used to decorate sketchbooks or notebooks

74. Drawn on boots before applying shoe polish

75. Drawn in the dirt before you wash your car

76. Drawn on lighters and matchboxes

77. Anointed on yourself

78. Drawn on important dates on the calendar

79. Painted on something that will assist your sigil at a paint-your-own-pottery studio

80. Drawn on the cleaning bucket or spray before cleaning your space

81. Carved into ice cubes

82. Flushed down the toilet

83. Buried in a place of honor

84. Drawn on the tools of your craft (whether magic or art)

85. Drawn on the cloth you use to clean your glasses

86. Drawn on your car

87. Drawn on your holiday decorations

88. Drawn on tarot cards

89. Drawn in secret places

90. Drawn on witch bottles

91. Drawn on a keychain

92. Drawn on the inside of a beverage sleeve

93. Drawn on your coffee cup when you're on the go

94. Drawn on your plane, train, or bus ticket

95. Drawn on old checks before destroying them

96. Anointed with water on your familiar (don't use oils or anything other than water, just to be safe)

97. Drawn on a bedpost

98. Carved into a pumpkin at Halloween

99. Carved into a yule log

"SHOULD I MAKE THIS SIGIL?"

There will (or should) be a lot of times when you question whether you should make a sigil for something, or whether you should cast a spell. Magic is controlling energy and taking action to change the world around you. You shouldn't be flippant about any spells you do, because you don't know what kind of effects there might be (short-term, long-term, or permanent). There have been some interesting side effects to a lot of spells I've cast. I have cast spells when I shouldn't have, and I've had to break the spell. I have made sigils that I had no business in making, and I've had to text my husband to destroy and banish the sigil.

I don't recommend casting spells if you're in an emotional state. Emotions are volatile, whether it's extreme happiness, sadness, anger, or lust. Consider the kinds of things you've wanted to do when you've been extremely emotional. Maybe you've wanted to break a window, or graffiti something, or hurt another person. If you follow through on certain acts, there's a bell that cannot be unrung. It might feel good at the time, but then in hindsight you might find yourself thinking, *Oh, shit. That was a bad idea.* Magic is not without consequences. As with anything we do in our lives, there is always the possibility of major consequences and the chance that something will be permanently changed. I think about the allegory of the toothpaste tube in relation to spreading rumors or saying something hurtful: it's really easy to squeeze out all of that toothpaste, but if you have to get it back in the tube, you're going to find it extremely difficult. It might even feel impossible. And no matter what, you're never going to be able to completely undo the damage done. This allegory is true for magic, too.

I'm not here to tell you to never do anything while feeling emotional. I'm not here to tell you to not do anything that results in damage. I regularly cast my fair share of hexes, and I am good at it. I'm here to tell you to be very conscious of the decisions you make, and be prepared to undo spells if it comes to it.

There might be a lot of instances in your magic practice where you find yourself wondering *Should I do this?*

The fact you are questioning indicates that you do need to consider the outcome, and that maybe you shouldn't do the act. Magic should always be approached with certainty. If you're not certain, the magic probably isn't going to work. If it works, it will be weak magic.

If you're uncertain because you're not sure what the results will be, take some time to ask the spirits questions, pull tarot cards, or use a pendulum to divine whether you should do something and what the outcome will be. Sometimes you'll even feel certain about doing something, but the foreseen results are so questionable that you'll change your mind, or reevaluate how you're going to go about it. For example, I was going to evoke an entity. I decided to pull some cards to see what I should conjure an entity for, and the cards were all strong *no* cards. I pulled one last card to just confirm—*Should I do this? Is it a good idea?*—and the card pulled was a reversed card that gave a clear answer that it would be a regrettable decision—a decision with livable results, but a regrettable decision nonetheless. I listened and opted to not evoke anything.

Divinatory tools are always a good ally to get answers around whether something is a good idea or not. Even if you're not a person who believes in spirits, or you don't think that divination tools are communicating with something else, they are assets in your magic because at the very least, they connect you to your subconscious and reveal what you're not seeing. Tarot, for example, is a mirror. That mirror can reveal a lot, just as holding up a painting or drawing to a mirror can reveal what you need to change or fix, or what isn't quite right.

Goal and Outcome Tarot Spread

These spreads are quick and easy divinations to determine whether the magic you want to do is a good idea or if the outcome will be what you're hoping for. This can help you decide whether or not to make a sigil or help determine if you need to tweak something before going through with the magic.

Draw two cards. The first represents why you want to create a sigil; the second represents your intention for the sigil. These cards can be pulled at random, or you can go through the deck and find two cards that resonate with you.

Three possible outcomes. Draw three, flip one. The one you flip is the outcome of the sigil. Based on this information, you can choose to follow through with the sigil, or regroup entirely.

CARDS TO REPRESENT THE SIGIL YOU WISH TO CREATE

DRAW THREE FLIP ONE

FOR EXAMPLE~ SAY ONE WISHES TO CREATE A SIGIL FOR SUCCESS IN NEW VENTURES

2 OF WANDS
making plans, vision

3 OF PENTACLES
building, progress

4 OF PENTACLES
(REVERSED)

maybe not $$$ in success, but stability and happiness

the remaining cards don't matter

SHOALING

A shoal is a large group of animals, usually fish. Gordon White (of the *Rune Soup* podcast and blog) wrote about the idea of shoaling sigils in 2010, and it's a brilliant idea:

> Regardless, shoaling seems to me quite a good metaphor for multi-sigil experiments because you have the whole ocean/unconscious, "firing it off into the depths" thing. . . . But you also have predation in the form of your conscious intellect. Presumably, you want your sigils to cluster somewhere that allows them to take root and possibly feed.

To shoal your sigils is to target what you want but be vague about it, kind of like casting a large net. For example, instead of making a sigil for money, you make sigils for a bunch of possibilities that hit the same target (pay raise for your spouse, getting more clients, getting more tips, etc.). The vagueness and openness allow for more opportunities to succeed. It basically creates a greater likelihood of the desired outcome.

Now, you sprinkle in "nice to haves" that are unrelated to your larger objective. These can be as grandiose or as small as you want. Having variety never hurts, either. Clear skin, saving money at the grocery store, someone finding a cure for cancer, whatever.

Now, create your sigils on a piece of paper in groups of four or more goals (like a shoal of fish). Once created, you can do whatever you want with them. White creates the sigils intuitively and burns the paper when he's done. But you do whatever you need to help you focus your energy and believe that the magic is going to happen.

Shoaling basically creates the likelihood that something is going to happen. Sometimes the outcome might be an intermingling of the results of two sigils, which is pretty neat. I create a lot of my shoals by embroidering a collection of sigils on a piece of cloth. The combination of methodical embroidery and shoaling seems to yield an extremely powerful outcome (this book's existing is a testament to that).

USING SIGILS TO CONJURE ENTITIES

In his book *Liber Null & Psychonaut*, Peter J. Carroll describes evocation, a means of conjuring entities (also called servitors) that can be performed by forming a sigil. Evocation is the art of creating or contacting entities, forming a relationship that allows the witch to conjure and command them. Entities can be spirits, elementals, familiars, demons, spirits, or any kind of noncorporeal being. These entities, once conjured, can be bound to anything or anyone, or they can be left to move around freely in the Aether, charged with fulfilling a particular task. They can bring change to the witch, to another person, or to the universe. The entity will go about and fulfill its task, independent from the witch or magician, until the job is done, at which point the entity will disappear. If at any time the entity needs to be banished, the magician can do so by destroying the sigil and banishing the entity from their mind.

The benefit to working with an entity in this way is that they are capable of making decisions and can adapt themselves to the task in a way that nonconscious spells cannot, and thus they are able to complete the most difficult or complex of requirements as they evolve.

An entity can be conjured based on preexisting knowledge, such as from a grimoire of spirits or demons, in which case you can use preexisting sigils or seals that represent the desired being. On the other hand, such entities can also be created entirely by the magician based on their needs or desires. A way to do this successfully is to create a sigil that combines the attributes of the entity you're trying to summon: their physical appearance, name, and other characteristics. Think of the attributes as spell ingredients that can be assembled. If you're evoking a being to help you develop psychic powers, you might draw a crescent moon for subconscious and psychic ability, an eye to represent second sight, a Pisces or Neptune symbol to represent intuition. Once you've selected your symbols, you combine them into one sigil, reworking the shape until it feels magical and powerful. You can also incorporate automatic drawing or writing to determine symbols and shapes to include in your servitor's sigil.

Be conscious of the entity you are conjuring, and charge the sigil by meditating on it until you feel it come to life. Keep the sigil on a piece of paper, in case you need to banish or destroy the servitor before its task is completed.

After you have evoked your servitor, be sure to cleanse yourself and reset your own energy. This type of work is mentally exhausting and energetically draining. You should also be sure to cleanse yourself and your space after banishing any servitors or entities that no longer serve you.

It's important to remember that this type of evocation is intense, powerful magic. It's not for the beginner witch or magician. Evoking entities requires diligence, caution, and certainty. There is always the risk of conjuring something you didn't intend to, and you don't want to be left with anything or anyone unsavory.

CANDLE MAGIC

Candle magic is an easy, practical, and straightforward means of using sigils in spellwork.

Choose a candle color that corresponds with your intention. If you're unsure or in doubt, use a white candle. When choosing a candle, it's also important to note that the size of the candle will determine how long it will burn (and how long your spell will last). If you're in a situation where you can't burn a candle for very long, then you can opt for a smaller candle like a tealight or a birthday candle. Sometimes it can be worthwhile to opt for a longer-burning candle, because your patience and dedication can be a vital contribution to the spell.

Does material matter? It can. On one hand, every type of wax comes from the earth in some way. You can choose something that burns more cleanly, like beeswax, but if you're vegan that might not be appealing. Different candle materials have the potential of carrying different energy, and that can play a part in your spellwork, but it's not essential to consider what your candle is made of. At the end of the day, a white taper you buy from a grocery store is going to be as good as anything else.

Here are some correspondences for wax, should you choose to intentionally choose your candle based on material:

Beeswax: made by bees. Can be used in spells around nature, warmth, safety, curses/hexes (both inflicting and breaking), industriousness, production, fertility, abundance, sweetness, community, family.

Paraffin wax: made from materials that come from fossil fuels, i.e., ancient things from long ago. Can be used in spells around science, history, ancestors, past lives, creating something, transmutation, mysteries.

Other types of wax: come from plants in some way. Because of their relationship to earth (grown in dirt, nurtured by water), they'll combine all of the elements once burned (feeding fire using air), and you can use these candles for anything that pertains to the earth—which is any type of spellwork.

> *TIP:* If you're proficient or interested, you can always make your own candles for spellwork.

You have the option of cleansing your candle of other energy that might be clinging to it. This isn't essential, but as with any tool that was created by someone else, or handled by others before coming to you, it doesn't hurt. You can cleanse the candle with visualization, gently wash it with water (if you have magical water on hand, that's even better), or pass it through incense smoke.

Gather oils, herbs, and salts to anoint the candle, based on what will amplify your magic the most.

Charge the candle with your intention by holding it in your hands and visualizing the magic you want to take action.

Determine the sigil you will use for this candle. You can use one you've made before, one that someone has made for you, or a historical sigil, or take time now to make a sigil for your spell. Carve the sigil into your candle, using a sharp tool like a knife, a needle, or a nail.

You may also create an incantation that feels powerful and addresses the intention and goal of the spell. Don't use the same phrase that you used to create your sigil, if you used a word method. However, you can use similar key words. You could even create a mantra sigil to use as your incantation. Speak aloud this incantation while you anoint and dress your candle, and while you light it.

Anoint the candle. Start by rubbing oil onto the candle, starting from the middle and going outward (middle to the wick, and middle to the base of the candle). Olive oil is a good oil for this, but you can use any oil. You can also choose to make a mix of essential oils for this purpose.

Dress the candle by rolling it in herbs and salt, or sprinkle the blend over the candle.

Light the candle while speaking your incantation or visualizing your spell taking action.

If possible, leave the candle burning until it is completely burned out. Pay attention to what it is doing. The way the candle burns can tell you how the spell is going. If it's burning evenly and the flame is holding steady, your spell is strong and stable. If the flame is erratic, or if there's a lot of smoke, the spell might be a bit unstable. If the flame extinguishes on its own before the candle has burned out or there is a lot of wax left over, you may need to reevaluate your spellwork. You don't need to read the flames or do anything beyond burning the candle. Sometimes a candle will act weird entirely because of your environment, and it has nothing to do with how the spell is going. If you want to be able to accurately read your candle flame, burn a control candle or two in the space in which you'll be burning your actual spell candle. This will give you an idea of any drafts or environmental factors that will influence the flame. Don't forget about your own body and the candle itself (wick length, wick-to-wax ratio, etc.) when considering environmental factors. Even with environmental factors, anything that the candle does is worth noting, if only for future reference.

Flame Meanings

Dancing/flickering: high energy, spiritual energy, high vibrations

High flame: powerful, strong spell

Weak flame: obstacles, weak spell, uncertainty

Blue flame: strong energy

Dual flame: another presence has entered the spell, disruption

Popping/cracking: spirits are trying to communicate

Curling wick: good sign

Candle won't stay lit: cease the spell, reevaluate, and try again

Candle burns quickly: spell is taking quick action, but it will likely be short-lived

Candle burns slowly: good sign of spellworking, but there may be some obstacles that will slow things down

Candle is destroyed: cease the spell, and do not try again

While it's best to leave the candle burning, fire safety is important. Don't leave candles unattended. Don't leave candles on a surface that will break or burn. I haven't quite burned my house down, but I've definitely done my fair share of damage while burning spell candles, including having a candle crack a plate right in half. If you need to let a candle burn through and it's going to take some time, leave it in a metal sink and away from anything flammable. If you're nervous or unsure, burn a smaller candle that you can see through to the end.

EMOJIS

If you introduce your sigil into a digital space, you can incorporate emoji spells to amplify the sigil. Emojis can have a lot of meanings, based on your own interpretations, what the emoji is universally understood to mean, what the emoji is used for, and what the emoji was made to represent.

Money symbols, money bags, nazar, diamonds, etc.—there's a lot of potential for magic. That's why so many craft emoji spells in general—they're a wonderful method of creating spells for the digital space in which we so often reside.

Plus, your phone is a powerful portal. Use those emojis and other digital tools in your magic!

Fun fact: I have created sigils using a notepad app when I was in a pinch, and the sigil worked *really* well. I think it helped that I was making a sigil for something that involved computers and digital technology. I was able to make a sigil that spoke the same language and existed in the same realm as what I needed to work.

INCORPORATE SIGILS INTO YOUR ART

While you don't want to share the literal meaning of your sigil, you can incorporate it into your art. This may mean building your artwork around the shape of a sigil, or painting a sigil onto a canvas and then painting over top of it. You can make your sigils as public or as secret as you choose. Sigils themselves are works of art. They are something you have crafted. It can be really beautiful to incorporate this into your art practice, whether it's big or small, secret or visible.

EMBROIDERING SIGILS AS A MEANS OF CHARGING

I would be remiss if I wrote an entire book on sigil crafting and didn't mention embroidering sigils. Not only are you going to yield a beautiful and mindfully created object, but you will charge your sigils in a really potent way. Whenever I need a really powerful charge or need to focus extra energy into my sigils, I hand-embroider them onto fabric. Oftentimes I'll even embroider a shoal or group of sigils. It takes a long time. I have calluses on my fingers. But it's a potent type of magic, which is why I return to it. It helps that needlework is already one of my passions.

The thing about embroidery is that you don't need anything fancy, and it's ultimately an inexpensive thing to do. A small skein of embroidery thread and a package of embroidery needles are all you need, and they can be had for a few dollars. You can get an inexpensive hoop, too, but depending on what you're embroidering, it's not really essential.

You can embroider any fabric, even something you wear every day. You can embroider a pillowcase with a sigil for a restful sleep, or a denim jacket with a sigil for protection. You can embroider secret sigils on the lining of coats, the inside of pants pockets, or on underwear.

Embroidery is steady and mindful, and it has the potential to pull your body into the sigil. You might accidentally prick your fingers and draw blood. You might lick the thread when threading your needle. While embroidering, focus your intention and think about the energy you're putting into this object. Focus on what the sigil is going to accomplish and achieve.

Some of the strongest sigils I've created have been charged through embroidery, complete with blood and saliva. My fingers are callused from all of the needlework I do, which reminds me of what a powerful witch I am and the very real things I am able to conjure.

Anything slowly and mindfully crafted is potent magic. It is also an act of rebellion and resilience to do something slowly. Our society doesn't reward or value slowness, but the act of performing methodical tasks like embroidery, mending, or baking bread pulls in another level of magic that will never be able to be purchased or manufactured. Consider that there are types of embroidery stitches that cannot be replicated by machines.

TAROT SPREAD TO CREATE A PERSONAL SYMBOL

This tarot spread creates a portrait of you, so that you can create a personal sigil to represent you. This sigil can be used as a power symbol, an art signature, or as a base for a self-portrait, or it can represent you in spells that focus on you. You can also use this spread to create a symbol for another person, pet, adversary, or deity, or to determine the attributes of an entity you're wishing to evoke. There are so many ways to use this spread, including using it as a means to check in with yourself.

CARD 1: How others see you

CARD 2: What matters to you

CARD 3: What scares you

CARD 4: Your talent

CARD 5: Your weakness

CARD 6: Your subconscious

CARD 7: Your aura

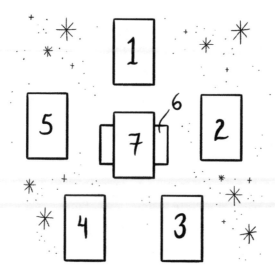

Once the reading is completed, you can proceed to making a sigil through a couple of means:

Option 1: Take the numbers from each card and put them into a magic square. Draw and connect the numbers in the order the cards were pulled. If the cards you're using don't have numbers, you could convert a key letter from each card into a number. If you choose this method, you could choose a square based on your sun sign, the day of the week you were born, or what planet means the most to you. The choice is yours, but as with all sigil crafting, the decision should be intentional.

Option 2: Determine a keyword for each card you pulled, for a total of seven words. Create a sigil using the Austin Osman Spare written method around those words.

Option 3: Gather up the cards and then scatter them, letting them fall in a random order. Using the lots method (on page 112), draw a shape connecting each card. You could connect the lines intuitively, or start with the first card and go in order of how the cards were pulled.

CORRESPONDENCES

Correspondences are magical associations that act as a connection from one thing to another. Literally, a correspondence is a similarity, an equivalent, or a connection. When we use correspondences, it's a type of sympathetic magic, in which we use equivalents to call on something that we can't yet access physically. We create correspondences in relation to planets, deities, emotions, and all kinds of other things. A simplified way to think of correspondences and to help make your own is to think about holidays or celebrations. For example, there are specific tastes, smells, sights, and symbols that you associate with Halloween: pumpkins, ghosts, cinnamon, candy corn, and maybe a hundred other things. The same goes when you think of a family member or a loved one. There are likely associations you make with this person: things they like, favorite colors, symbols that connect with a specific memory, a special dish they made. These symbol associations are correspondences.

Now, instead of associating things with a person or a holiday, think about what you connect with magical things. When you think of abundance, what comes to mind? When you think of your zodiac sign, what images are conjured? The correspondences you use can come from your own intuitive reactions, or they can be predetermined, like something you learned from a friend, a book, or your culture. All are valid.

This section is a reference to help you determine the best way to make a sigil, what planets to work with, and what components you might incorporate into a spell to amplify the sigil you've created (for example, if you want to create a spell for abundance, you might use the Sun square to make a sigil and then carve that sigil into a gold candle). Refer back to it when you're stuck in any spellwork, or you're feeling curious.

As with anything in this world, these correspondences only begin to scratch the surface of what can be used to work with different planets. Use your intuition to develop your own correspondences. The connections you make between planets and other things may surprise you, and those connections that come from your own being and personal history make for some strong and powerful magic.

Types of Spells and Corresponding Ingredients

This section offers some options for spell ingredients to use in spellwork. I have organized the correspondences by type of spell, from success to love spells to curses. Cast spells based on your own needs and desires, but before you start casting spells on other people, consider ethics. I do not believe that we should avoid curses or hexes. There are valid reasons for needing to cast certain types of spells, and no one should be condemned for wanting, or needing, to use magic for those reasons.

The most ethically questionable form of spellcasting involves love spells. I advise against casting spells to make someone fall in love with you. By all means, cast spells to help you love yourself or to help you find the right partner. But avoid spells that target someone's free will.

If casting a spell feels like a bad idea, listen to that instinct. Don't cast spells that you might regret.

Also, remember that these correspondences are suggestions, based on my own experiences and research. Make your own correspondences. Find spell ingredients that work for you, and make note of them in this book.

Money / Abundance / Manifestation / Success

yellow, gold (for success, manifestation), green, brown (growth, abundance), money symbols, gold coins, gold icons, cows, grains, rabbits, sunflowers, money, found pennies, old checks, ants, bees, grasshopper, jade, keys, new moon, waxing moon, full moon, moon in Taurus, moon in Virgo, moon in Capricorn, sunstone, pyrite, citrine, 10 of Pentacles, 10 of Cups, Emperor, the sun

Air for movement and creativity

Earth for growth

Fire for energy, to speed things up

Water for getting things to flow, cash flow

Love / Self-Love / Sex Magic

red, pink, condoms, lube, sex toys, candy, candy hearts, cinnamon hearts, copper, coral, bees, rose, knots, Valentine's Day or other dates significant to love, the numbers 1 and 2, full moon, dark moon for self-love and self-care, moon in Taurus, moon in Virgo, moon in Scorpio, heart shape, peach, plum, vanilla, rings, east and west winds, chile pepper, cinnamon, clove, columbine, cats/feline energy, ruby, emerald, rhodonite, rhodochrosite, chrysoprase, rose quartz, oysters, oyster shells, conch shells, orchid, vervain, the Lovers, Knight of Cups, 2 of Cups, the Star, Venus, Aphrodite, Friday

Water for emotions

Earth for grounding into the body and earthly pleasures

Fire for passion

To Curse / to Hex

ashes, chain, black, red, shower/sink drain, knife, knots, dark moon, moon in Aries, moon in Scorpio, black pepper, rubber bands, thread/cord, vinegar, precision, herringbone, evil eye, basil, bryony, vetch, pins, the Tower, 3 of Swords, 8 of Swords, urine, feces, dead insects, toilet, mud, cemetery dirt, burying, blood, menstrual blood, blood, Mars, Tuesday

Fire for destruction, speed

To Break Curses / Hexes

animal heart full of pins, quicksilver/mercury, horseshoe, snake essence, angelica, betony, birch, oregano, plantain, wild rue, field wormwood, holy thistle, thistle, black, gray, the Tower (reversed), Death card, mirror, black cloth, salt

Water and Air for cleansing

Protection

bay, betony, birch, broom, buckthorn, chrysanthemum, black hellebore, juniper, mugwort, oregano, pimpernel, sage, summer savory, devil's bit, strawberry, basil thyme, black, fences, chain, locks, barbed wire, garlic, topaz, dark moon, new moon, cone shells, rowan, Queen of Wands, Queen of Swords, black tourmaline, obsidian, smoky quartz, onyx

Luck

found objects (especially pennies), rabbit's foot, mandrake, date palm, bamboo, daylight hours, horseshoe, yellow, gold, brown, agate, jade, quartz, the sun, Four of Wands, clover (especially four-leaf clover), Jupiter

Healing

aloe, essence of red cabbage, catnip, cowslip, marshmallow, peony, bandages, ankh, foods associated with feeling better (like chicken noodle soup, ginger ale, herbal teas), green, white, gray, pastels, vervain, Hermit card, Temperance, the Star, mugwort, thistle, thyme, amethyst, lepidolite, lithium quartz, moldavite

Water and Air for emotional cleaning and clearing

Psychic Powers/Intuition

agaric, bay, wormwood, moon in Pisces, full moon, dark moon, blue, purple, gray, the Magician, High Priestex, the moon, cinnamon, mugwort, quartz, lapis lazuli, labradorite, selenite

Communicating with Spirits

pendulum, Ouija boards, alder, asphodel, banyan, barley, bistort, clove, moon in Pisces, full moon, dark moon, purple, black, the moon, the High Priestex, yew, mugwort, dandelion, wormwood, apophyllite, kyanite, Saturn

Changing Habits/Setting Goals/Personal Growth

green, purple, left-handed whelks, Wheel of Fortune, the Devil, Ace of Wands, the Fool, moldavite, kyanite, malachite, rutilated quartz, aventurine

Courage/Strength/Soothing Anxiety

fern, oak, peach, peony, red, Strength card, mullein, black cohosh, yarrow, carnelian, aragonite

Peace/Calm

blue, white, dulse, pennyroyal, vervain, lavender, howlite, amethyst, celestite, apophyllite

Banishing

ash, broom, chicory, dark moon, waning moon, black, soap and water, toilet, drain, counterclockwise movement, pentagram, Death card, angelica, basil, garlic, juniper, pepper, rosemary, sage, yarrow, black salt, salt, moon in Aries, Tuesday, Mars

Protection When Traveling

old-man's beard, malachite, black tourmaline, Mercury

Planetary and Celestial Correspondences

In the magic-square method, there are seven squares, as described by Henry Cornelius Agrippa in the sixteenth century, and later illustrated by Francis Barrett in his 1801 book, *The Magus*. Each of these seven squares corresponds to a celestial body. Generally speaking, these seven bodies are referred to as "planets," although it is technically incorrect. You may also be thinking about how there are more than seven planets in our solar system.

When Agrippa's *Three Books of Occult Philosophy* was written, there were only eight known celestial bodies known to mankind, including Earth. The other seven "planets" were the sun, the moon, Mercury, Venus, Mars, Jupiter, and Saturn. While modern astrologers take all known planets into account (as well as certain asteroids and comets), most magical practitioners don't concern themselves with the more distant planets. Supposedly, this is because they are too far away to affect our spellwork, or because they're too volatile. Personally, I wouldn't be surprised if it were because of a more mundane reason. Maybe trying to make magic squares for all of the celestial bodies is just too complicated, or they get too big. Maybe no one has tried, because seven planets are enough.

For the sake of simplicity, I'll refer to the celestial bodies colloquially as planets.

Within the realm of sigil crafting, we use the seven aforementioned planets. Each planet has its own house of expertise, working better for some types of magic and spellwork than others. Generally, you'll be able to work with any planet, but the results might be drastically different, or the magic will happen in weird and unexpected ways. For example, Jupiter is expansive, so working with it for money or growth is a great idea! But Jupiter may not be the best planet to work with if you're looking to minimize or let go.

These correspondences are intended to offer some information on the different planets, in order to amplify your sigils that work with the magic squares assigned to each planet. While they do not have planetary squares, I have included correspondences for Earth, Uranus, Neptune, and Pluto, should you want to work with them in your sigil crafting and spellwork.

For the sun, moon, Mercury, Venus, Mars, Jupiter, and Saturn, I have also included their planetary hours. These are the times of day that are ruled by each planet, cycling through each planet every seven hours. You can use these times to amplify your sigil that is based on a particular planet's square. For example, if you wanted to work with the sun for a success or abundance sigil, you might choose to make and/or charge the sigil on Sunday, at 0900. If you're making a sigil to use in a curse, you might choose to use the Mars square, creating and charging your sigil on Tuesday at 0100 or 1500.

I have chosen to offer the planetary hours in military time, as this twenty-four-hour clock can help remove any confusion regarding morning versus afternoon. It is also important to note that the planetary hour is relative to the time zone you are in (for example, if you're in a moon hour, another part of the world will be in a Mercury hour at the same moment).

Sun

works of light, wealth, truth, identity, individuality, success, abundance, manifestation

cedar, chamomile, chrysanthemum, copal, frankincense, goldenseal, juniper, oak, orange, rowan, St. John's Wort, sunflower, tangerine, lion, rooster, Queen of Wands, the sun, 10 of Pentacles, 10 of Cups, Strength, gold, chimera, phoenix, Leo, bay, heliotropes, cinnamon, chrysolite (peridot), ruby, gold, yellow, gold (metal), sunstone, pyrite, citrine, carnelian, Apollo, Ra, clear quartz, vanadinite, tiger's eye, Sunday

PLANETARY HOURS:

Sunday 0100, 0900, 1500, 2200

Monday 0500, 1200, 1900

Tuesday 0200, 0900, 1600, 2300

Wednesday 0600, 1300, 2000

Thursday 0300, 1000, 1700, 0000

Friday 0700, 1400, 2100

Saturday 0400, 1100, 1800

Moon (Entire Moon, Regardless of Phase)

divination, mysteries, conjuration of spirits, necromancy (divination with Spirits), faith, emotions, feelings, subconscious

aloe, Irish moss, lettuce, lotus, lily, moonwort, willow, the sea, tides, heavy rain, silver cloth, silver (metal), clubmoss, Luna, Selene, owl, catfish, cats, Bast, Diana, Artemis, water, circle, crescent shape, divination, white, black, gray, blue, pearls, white sandalwood, camphor, mugwort, selenotropes, coyotes, wolves, hazel, almond, Cancer, the moon, High Priestess, crab, shells, moonstone, selenite, apophyllite, apatite, sodalite, Monday

PLANETARY HOURS:

Sunday 0400, 1100, 1800

Monday 0100, 0800, 1500, 2200

Tuesday 0500, 1200, 1900

Wednesday 0200, 0900, 1600, 2300

Thursday 0600, 1300, 2000

Friday 0300, 1000, 1700

Saturday 0700, 1400, 2100

New Moon and Waxing Moon

planting seeds, setting intentions, growth, preparation, insemination, creative spark

seeds, eggs, lithium quartz, Herkimer diamonds, semen, the Fool, the Magician, Ace of Cups, Ace of Wands, apple seeds, cut apple, flower starting to bloom

Full Moon

embodiment, fulfillment, paying attention, energy, duality, illumination, celebration

fireflies, kunzite, fluorite, clear quartz, Herkimer diamond, cauldron, pregnancy

Waning Moon and Dark Moon

rest, renewal, transformation, rebirth, death, banishing, protection, quiet

howlite, black, lodolite quartz, shungite, lepidolite, labradorite, smoky quartz, low tide, black salt, ash, Death, bones, Ragana, cats (especially black or gray cats), black panthers, Bast, Lilith, Hecate, heather

Mercury

intelligence, communication, works of skill, science, eloquence, travel, networking, knowledge, information

agaric, aspen, flax, horehound, mandrake, summer savory, eyebright, lily of the valley, mustard (especially black), rue, nonbinary, androgynous, trans, quicksilver, silver-colored things, wings, clouds, fabric or surfaces that change color, iridescence, agate, science, science equipment, green, reflections, mirror, telephone, the Magician,

8 of Wands, swallow, sparrow, carrier pigeon, Gemini, Virgo, Mercury, Apollo, chrysocolla, hemimorphite, lapis lazuli, blue lace agate, blue kyanite, labradorite, stork, Wednesday

PLANETARY HOURS:

Sunday 0300, 1000, 1700, 0000

Monday 0700, 1400, 2100

Tuesday 0400, 1100, 1800

Wednesday 0100, 0800, 1500, 2200

Thursday 0500, 1200, 1900

Friday 0200, 0900, 1600, 1100

Saturday 0600, 1300, 2000

Venus

love, marriage, beauty, charity, sex, desire, relationships, harmony, unity, eroticism

apple, aster, bleeding heart, catnip, columbine, daffodil, foxglove, hibiscus, Venus flytrap, white, green, pink, pastels, nude/naked body, dove, Friday, goat, emerald, copper (especially polished copper), roses, myrtle, swan feathers, swan, Venus, Aphrodite, the sea, nature, leaves, grass, seashells, oysters, pearl, pastels, apricot, pink geranium, iris, Taurus, Libra, the Empress, the Lovers, 2 of Cups, 3 of Cups, Queen of Cups, rose quartz, dioptase, rhodonite, rhodochrosite, Friday

PLANETARY HOURS:

Sunday 0200, 0900, 1600, 2300

Monday 0600, 1300, 2000

Tuesday 0300, 1000, 1700, 0000

Wednesday 0700, 1400, 2100

Thursday 0400, 1100, 1800

Friday 0100, 0800, 1500, 2200

Saturday 0500, 1200, 1900

Mars

works of anger, punishment, justice, curses, hexes, communication with spirits of those who were killed, will, drive, determination, banishment

bloodroot, chile pepper, dragon's blood, gentian, hawthorn, houndstongue, nettle, wormwood, witch grass, ebony, brown, red, fire, wolves, vulture, iron, sword, shield, justice, Ares, Mars, color of fire, the color of rust, the color of blood, steel, warhorse, weaponry, ram, owl, scarlet, Aries, Scorpio, carnelian, tiger's eye, garnet, the Emperor, the Tower, 5 of Wands, 5 of Swords, Tuesday

PLANETARY HOURS:

Sunday 0700, 1400, 2100

Monday 0400, 1100, 1800

Tuesday 0100, 0800, 1500, 2200

Wednesday 0500, 1200, 1900

Thursday 0200, 0900, 1600, 2300

Friday 0600, 1300, 2000

Saturday 0300, 1000, 1700, 0000

Jupiter

ambition, politics, luck, fortune, expansion, charity, money

borage, dandelion, fig, sarsaparilla, sage, alfalfa, allspice, banyan, be-still, bluebell, camellia, iron, lightning, thunder, bull, stag, eagle, tin, pentagram, blue, oak, fig tree, the sky, Wheel of Fortune, Sagittarius, Pisces, merlinite, jade, aragonite, 2 of Wands, 3 of Pentacles, 3 of Wands, Thursday

PLANETARY HOURS:

Sunday 0600, 1300, 2000

Monday 0300, 1000, 1700, 0000

Tuesday 0700, 1400, 2100

Wednesday 0400, 1100, 1800

Thursday 0100, 0800, 1500, 2200

Friday 0500, 1200, 1900

Saturday 0200, 0900, 1600, 2300

Saturn

protection against sickness, protection against deception, death, communicating the dead, conjuring the dead and Spirits, authority, responsibility, limitations, restrictions, time, tradition

belladonna, buckthorn, cypress, hemlock, hellebore, mullein, wolf's bane, heather, yew, barren earth, salt, black salt, white beard, black, brown, juniper, hook, sickle, scythe, lead, cane, shed snakeskin, dried blood, sulfur, onyx, ash, indigo, Saturn, Cronos, watch, hourglass, sand, amethyst, obsidian, jet, black tourmaline, onyx, hematite, Aquarius, Capricorn, Death, Judgment, Hierophant, 10 of Swords, Saturday

PLANETARY HOURS:

Sunday 0500, 1200, 1900

Monday 0200, 0900, 1600, 2300

Tuesday 0600, 1300, 2000

Wednesday 0300, 1000, 1700, 0000

Thursday 0700, 1400, 2100

Friday 0400, 1100, 1800

Saturday 0100, 0800, 1500, 2200

Earth

Earth generally isn't considered in spellwork, but Earth is our parent and our home. So it is worth considering how we can work with our planet in direct ways. Anything and everything that is created on or by the Earth can act as a correspondence, but here are a few that I thought of: jasper (all types), Taurus, Taurean energy, cannabis, dirt, salt, your own body

Uranus

originality, technology, change, individuality, electricity, invention, independence, unconventional, unexpected, sudden change, upheaval, revolution, releasing tradition, thinking creatively, embracing the unusual

jade, blue topaz, black tourmaline, labradorite, the Fool, the Tower, the Devil, Aquarius, air, breaking something down to rebuild (like creating a mosaic out of broken items)

Neptune

impression, shifting, spiritual and psychic matters, dreams, depth, mystic, esoteric, fluidity, intuition, confusion tridents, dolphins, sea creatures (especially dark and mysterious sea creatures, like angler fish), octopus, lapis lazuli, Angelite, danburite, the moon, Pisces

Pluto

change, transformation, secrets, undercover information, release, destruction, rebirth, renewal

purple, black, rutilated quartz, malachite, sugilite, moldavite, amethyst, key, pomegranate, Hades, Scorpio, Death, the Hermit, 3 of Swords

Elemental Correspondences

Air

change, creativity, movement

open window, east, fans, feathers, leaves, clouds, birds, windy places, fairies, sprites, pastels, Gemini, Libra, Aquarius

Earth

grounding, growth, harvest

salt, grains, herbs, maps, globe, atlas, north, nature, mountains, gnomes, dwarves, Taurus, brown, Virgo, Capricorn

Fire

passion, drastic change, energy, illumination

salamanders, south, summer, matches, incense, candles, fireplaces, red, orange, the Sun, fire dragons, phoenix, Aries, Leo, Sagittarius

Water

emotions, healing, cleansing, unconscious

west, the moon, blue, green, seashells, photos of the sea, saltwater, whales, fish, mermaids, Cancer, Scorpio, Pisces

Color Correspondences

Pink

love, body, friendship, gender fuckery, affection, compassion, gentleness, romance, softness, Taurus, Libra, Venus

Red

passion, aggression, attention, birth, blood, sexuality, love, vigor, sex, stop, war, root, Aries, Leo, Scorpio, Mars

Orange

encouragement, confidence, creativity, energy, warmth, harvest, autumn, attraction, stimulation, sex, sexuality, sacral, Leo, Mercury

Yellow

changing minds, caution, anxiety, cowardice, gold, optimism, positivity, sunshine, wisdom, solar plexus, power, Gemini, Leo, Sun

Green

money, luck, financial success and prosperity, fertility, good crops and harvest, go, creativity, abundance, life, love, healing, heart, envy, Taurus, Libra, Capricorn, Virgo, Pisces, Venus

Blue

calm, communication, throat, awareness, third eye, divine, water, flow, intellect, reflection, sadness, peace, understanding, spirituality, awareness, Aquarius, Cancer, Virgo, Taurus, Libra, Sagittarius, Neptune

Purple

ambition, psychic ability, spirituality, crown, introspection, intuition, inspiration, royalty, wisdom, Sagittarius, Jupiter

Brown

complex, grounding, hard work, humility, nourishment, organic, practicality, death, warmth, stability, structure, Capricorn, Virgo, earth

Black

sadness and mourning, protection, confidence, creation, death, elegance, gravity, rebellion, sophistication, shadow energy, space, internal, Capricorn, Saturn, Pluto

Gray

neutrality, duality, complex, fluid, scale, nonbinary, spectrum, Moon

White

spiritual strength, breaks curses or crossed conditions, faith, purity, truth, sincerity, peace, cleanliness, coldness, bone, skeleton, death, ghosts, isolation, minimalism, simplicity, truth, winter, moon

Days of the Week

Sunday

ruled by the sun

gods, raising vibration, gaining the favor of those in high places, riches, honor, glory, friendship, success, abundance, manifestation, creation, creativity

Monday

ruled by the moon

reconciliation, dreams, safe travel, messages, fertility (including creative fertility), divination, transitions, shapeshifting, finding truths

Tuesday

ruled by Mars

courage, overthrowing enemies, breaking negative spells, hexing, cursing, banishment

Wednesday

ruled by Mercury

psychic and spiritual development, communication, divination, influencing others, traveling, science, health, research, learning, studying

Thursday

ruled by Jupiter

wealth, success, fortune, obtaining good luck, health, expanding mind and ideas, ambition

Friday

ruled by Venus

love, romance, sex magic, beauty, happiness, gratifying lust, masturbation, self-care

Saturday

ruled by Saturn

protection spells (especially against psychic attacks), communication with spirits, death, renewal, rest, tradition, ancestor work

CONCLUSION

You don't need to be a witch or believe in "woo-woo" to use sigils.
Yes, a certain amount of belief is required, but that belief can be anything, including a belief that something is possible, and it can be made real. Belief is trust. Trust that what you desire is a possibility, and you deserve it. I'm not really all about positive mental attitudes or positive thinking, but that's because of my life with depression, anxiety, and the overwhelm that can come with undiagnosed ADHD. Realistically, thanks to cognitive behavioral therapy and counseling, I know that thinking affirmatively and in possibility (rather than impossibility) is at least a good thing for your brain. I'm not a therapist or a psychologist or an expert in anything (other than witchery and sigils), but it seems to be proven that brains like it when you tell them facts. You don't have to know if they're true. You just have to tell your brain that they are. Brains will unravel our uncertainties until we fall into pits of despair. But if we tell our brains a fact, an answer to its spiraling questions, our brain will calm down and then we'll calm down.

Something I was reading while working on this book was *Your Art Will Save Your Life* by Beth Pickens. Pickens addresses those inner dialogues that go through our heads, the lies that we tell ourselves. I like art books because they always feel magical, but they're based on real-life things, so to speak. A lot of the dialogue is what I see in witchcraft books. There's a similarity between our need for self-care and wellness and our desire for witchcraft or the metaphysical. That's a big part of why magic persists and will always persist. But sometimes we don't want magic. We want something that comes from the mundane world.

The word *mundane* comes from *mundi*, which means world. Mundane things are not separate from our selves or our magic. Magic is not separate from the mundane. Sometimes the best results do occur when we marry the two, when we find magic in the mundane, and the mundane in our magic.

Sigil crafting is a form of magic that meets the mundane, and there can be flux in that relationship. Sometimes sigils are fifty-fifty magical and mundane. Other times, the split is ninety-ten in favor of the mundane. This is why sigils hold so much potential for art as well as other applications. I might draw a sigil for something mundane, like getting an important document on time or saving money on groceries. I might use a sigil to evoke an entity. I might create a sigil to inspire or start an artwork.

If I don't make any other point in this book, I want to make this clear: sigils are varied and limitless. They are a technological marvel and a method to tap into our primordial core. Sigils are divine and mundane. They are witchcraft; they are illogical; they are mystical. And you don't have to believe in anything to use them beyond possibility and your own ability. There are no constraints in sigils. There is no initiation. There are no high doctrines you must understand. You don't need to be educated, from a particular background, or anything more than yourself as you are.

You just have to be willing to let them work and know that they will work.

SOME QUESTIONS YOU MIGHT HAVE

What if my sigil doesn't work? How long until I see results? Is this all nonsense? Why doesn't my magic seem to work?

Be patient. Trust in the process. We exist in a world where we want to see immediate effects, so we know at that moment that there will be a reward for our hard work. There's nothing wrong with that, but magic/God/Universe/Spirit doesn't function on our schedule. Time is a construct. Sometimes it will take time for our sigils to work; or when they do, they'll work in unexpected ways that fulfill our wish, but not in the way we wanted. Sometimes sigils won't work because we don't really believe they're going to work, or we don't give them enough power. There are countless reasons, and at the end of the day, if your sigil doesn't work, you have options.

If you don't see your desired results, check in. Do you really want what you're sigilizing? Do you really believe that it's your desire? Were you clear enough in your intention? Do you actually believe that you can access your desires? Have you done other magic that goes against your desires or sigils?

You have to believe. There can't be any doubt in your mind that your wish can come to fruition. Clear your mind, reevaluate, and reapproach.

Trust the mystery. Experiment. Be willing to fail. Be open to different results. Magic is wonderful and terrifying and marvelous and strange *because* it's unpredictable. We can control it, but it is organic and can act in ways we couldn't have expected. Think of magic as a dog. It may seem tame, but if something happens, you could get bitten, or you could receive a happy tail wag. You can do everything in your power to understand the theory, but at the end of the day, you just need to get out there and interact with it.

MAGIC IS REAL

As I mentioned in the introduction, this book exists because I make sigils. This book doesn't even scratch the surface of the success I've seen through using sigils in my day-to-day life and in my more complex rituals, not to mention the ways I've seen sigils help others, and the wild results they've had. If I told you everything, I don't know if you'd believe me. Still, it's because of my experience that I believe in sigils. And I believe in magic.

Magic is real. It's a complicated beast that I am grateful to have befriended.

Aleister Crowley described magic as "the science and art of causing change to occur in conformity with will." I think that Crowley's distillation of magic is astute and accurate, but in a lot of ways, it is an oversimplification. Thousands of ideas about what magic is and how it can be defined have been put forward by scholars and magicians and witch hunters, but they will never be entirely satisfactory. How can you truly summarize something as vast and as powerful as magic? We can make attempts, but magic is like love or excitement or frustration or homesickness. We can do our best to define it, but it will never justify the experience or the true feeling. Not everything is meant to be broken down into literal meanings. Not everything can be.

This book is my art, and I am grateful that I am able to share it with you. This book is also my magic, my craft, and my witchery. It covers a lot, but it's impossible to cover every aspect of magic. Every part of magic is so varied and vast, and it is tightly interwoven with human history and our individual experiences. We often want to brush off the concept of magic because it's illogical or there's no proof. Logic and proof aren't everything. If logic really ruled the world, our monetary systems would actually make sense and more politicians would be in prison (or at least impeached). Our world isn't a logical place, and we're not logical creatures, so why not lean into our intuition and our instincts and use magic?

I will always believe in magic, largely because it makes life more interesting. It is more inspiring to be open to the possibility of the weird and impossible. It's more fun to believe in fairies, UFOs, astral projection, spells, gods, cryptids, and unknown secrets. It's not interesting to grind your heels into fundamental skepticism. I don't try to explain or understand the things that happen to me or the wild reality I live in, but I know it to be true. When you open yourself up to possibility, the impossible stops seeming so impossible. I used to be a hard-set skeptic. But now, I'm a witch.

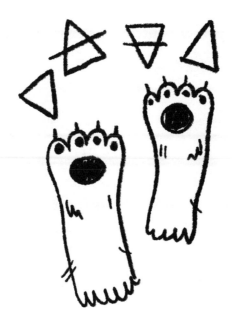

RECOMMENDED AND FURTHER READING

Pop Magic! by Grant Morrison

The Miracle Club by Mitch Horowitz

The Book of Pleasure by Austin Osman Spare

Liber Null and Psychonaut by Peter J. Carroll

Goodly Spellbook: Olde Spells for Modern Problems by Dixie Deerman
and Steven Rasmussen

Doctrine and Ritual of High Magic by Éliphas Lévi

Feels Good Man documentary

The Psychonaut Field Manual by Bluefluke

Your Art Will Save Your Life by Beth Pickens

GLOSSARY OF COMMON SYMBOLS

TRIANGLE	CIRCLE	SQUARE	ADD	SUBTRACT
MULTIPLY	DIVIDE	EQUALS	AIR	EARTH
FIRE	WATER	WATER	SPIRAL	LOVE
HAPPINESS	PEACE	MONEY	DAY	NIGHT
INFINITY	THEREFORE	YIN + YANG	CHAOS	SQUARED CIRCLE

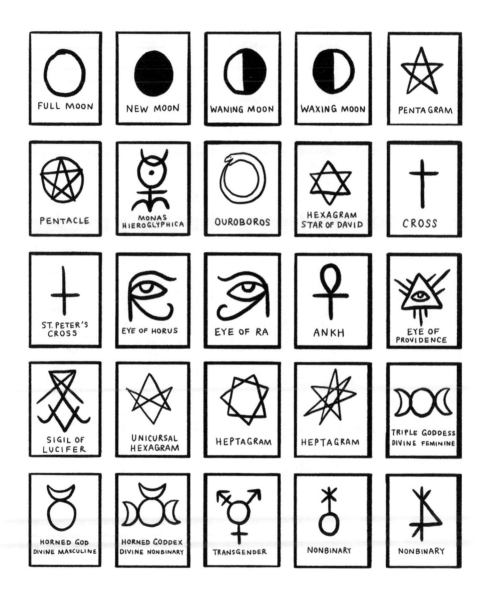

FULL MOON

NEW MOON

WANING MOON

WAXING MOON

PENTAGRAM

PENTACLE

MONAS HIEROGLYPHICA

OUROBOROS

HEXAGRAM STAR OF DAVID

CROSS

ST. PETER'S CROSS

EYE OF HORUS

EYE OF RA

ANKH

EYE OF PROVIDENCE

SIGIL OF LUCIFER

UNICURSAL HEXAGRAM

HEPTAGRAM

HEPTAGRAM

TRIPLE GODDESS DIVINE FEMININE

HORNED GOD DIVINE MASCULINE

HORNED GODDEX DIVINE NONBINARY

TRANSGENDER

NONBINARY

NONBINARY

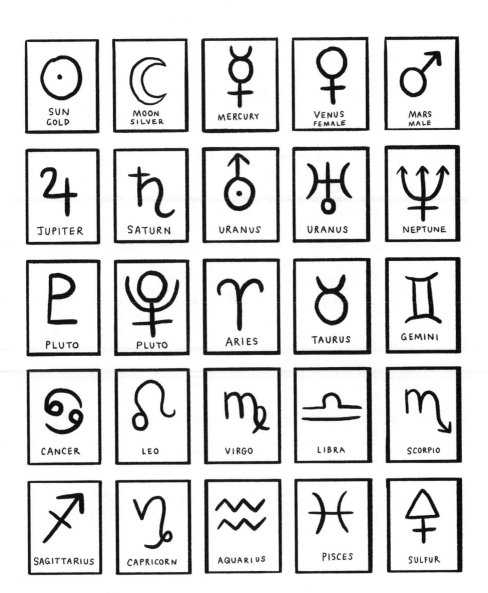

SULFUR

LEAD

IRON

TO PURIFY

ASHES

CRYSTAL

CRUCIBLE

CRUCIBLE

CRUCIBLE

SALT

SALT

JUSTICE

STAR

SKULL

USE THESE BLANK SPACES TO RECORD SYMBOLS THAT ARE IMPORTANT TO YOU!

ACKNOWLEDGMENTS

This book was written in New Brunswick, in the part of the province which includes the traditional unceded territories of the Wabanaki (Dawnland Confederacy), the Mi'kma'ki, and Wolastoqiyik (Maliseet). I am grateful to be a guest on this land, in a place where I can write books, make art, and make magic.

Thank you to so, so, so many people who helped make this book possible and kept cheering me on through the process.

INDEX

ABOUT THE AUTHOR

Lia Taylor (they/them) is a queer nonbinary multidisciplinary artist and witch. They graduated from the Alberta College of Art and Design (now Alberta University of the Arts) in 2014 with a bachelor's degree in fine art in fiber. Lia's true passion is traditional textile art, including weaving and embroidery. Their work explores the history of witchcraft, feminism, witches in pop culture, and the body. When they are not making art or researching witchcraft and witch trials, they are casting spells and conjuring all manners of witchery.

Lia likes movies, strong coffee, and cats.

CREATE YOUR OWN SIGILS

USE THESE PAGES TO MAKE YOUR OWN SIGILS!